W9-BCP-055

WHAT'S THAT PIG OUTDOORS?

WHAT'S THAT PIG OUTDOORS?

A Memoir of Deafness

HENRY KISOR

Foreword by Walker Percy

G.K.HALL&CO.

Boston, Massachusetts

1991

Published in Large Print by arrangement with
Hill and Wang, a division of
Farrar, Straus & Giroux.

British Commonwealth rights courtesy of A.M. Heath & Company, Ltd.

Portions of Chapter 9 originally appeared in the Chicago *Sun-Times*.

In the interest of privacy, the names of a few principals and places have been changed.

G. K. Hall Large Print Book Series.

Set in 18 pt. Plantin.

Library of Congress Cataloging-in-Publication Data

Kisor, Henry.
    What's that pig outdoors? : a memoir of deafness / Henry Kisor ;
foreword by Walker Percy.
        p.   cm.—(G.K. Hall large print book series)
    ISBN 0-8161-5113-X (lg. print)
    1. Kisor, Henry.   2. Deaf—United States—Biography.   3. Large type
books.   I. Title.
[HV2534.K57A3   1991]
362.4'2'092—dc20   90-19265
[B]

For Debby
who wouldn't rest till the book was done
and
for my parents
whose faith never flagged

FOREWORD

Here is a remarkable book. It is the autobiography of a man totally deaf since childhood. It is also the story of a man who
became a distinguished journalist.

It would be interesting on either count.
There are many autobiographies of deaf people and there are many autobiographies of
distinguished journalists. But this is the only
life story I have ever read of a deaf person
which is also written by a first-class writer.
The only exception is Helen Keller's *The
Story of My Life*, not really comparable because Helen of course was blind as well.

And it makes all the difference, the splendid writing. If for no other reason it would
be worth reading for the entertainment, a
lively tale told well—and often extremely
funny.

But what sets it apart and gives it its value
is not merely the story of a courageous person overcoming a serious handicap—though
it is this—but a moving account from a novel

perspective of the universal experience, which most of us take for granted, of the human breakthrough into language. Or what should be a universal human experience. For in fact some of the beneficiaries of this book could well be not only the deaf or the teachers of the deaf or the acquaintances of the deaf but so-called normal hearing people who have still not made the breakthrough into this kind of literacy.

There is a personal connection here. My daughter is also totally deaf. She and Henry are both remarkable for what they have achieved in a hearing world. But the connection is something else, someone else, an extraordinary, eccentric, and wonderful teacher whom you will meet in these pages.

A native genius, the teacher somehow had the wit—and I think Henry would agree—to go to the heart of the matter, not only of the education of deaf children but of human intelligence itself. Here is how Henry describes it. She (the Teacher, as we thought of her) arranged things with "parents placing their faces in the baby's line of vision"—yes, she'd start at eleven months—"so that the child could associate the movements of their lips with objects and actions." Here of course the Teacher hit upon what Helen

Keller had discovered in her own way, the unique human trick of symbolizing, of putting together the word and thing. Hers was, is, a revolutionary method which I think still has not received its due.

It is with her help and that of many others, with his own ebullience and good humor, with good teachers, good family, good wife, and plain guts that Henry Kisor not only made it but made it in high style—in spite of the knocks, some dumb teachers of the deaf, and such atrocities as "psychological testing."

Here, among other things, you will also learn about such mysteries as how it is deaf people know when someone comes into a room and says hello behind them. And you will learn much besides, with considerable delight and a kind of smiling wonderment.

WALKER PERCY

PREFACE

There's an old joke about three elderly deaf gentlemen, all lipreaders, aboard a train.

As it comes into a station, one looks out the window and says, "Ah, it's Weston."

"Wednesday?" says the second. "I thought it was Thursday."

"Thirsty?" says the third. "I am, too. Let's have a drink."

This tale illustrates a central truth of deafness: lipreading is full of snares and delusions. The term "lipreading" itself is technically a misnomer, for the act involves much more than merely watching movements of the lips. "Speechreading" is a more accurate term; some educators of the deaf call it "visual hearing." (I use "lipreading" here simply because it's the common term in the hearing world.) Broken into its components, lipreading seems an almost impossible circus trick, like juggling Indian clubs while spinning a dinner plate on one's forehead.

That story about the three old gents illustrates the biggest problem of lipreading: many sounds *look* identical. "M," "p," and "b" are made by bringing the lips together. "T," "d," and "l" all take shape with the tongue on the roof of the mouth just behind the teeth. As a result, the words, "bat," "bad," "ban," "mat," mad," "man," "pat," "pad," and "pan" all look exactly alike. To the eye there is no difference between "s" and "z." Sounds formed in the back of the throat are impossible to distinguish from one another. "Cat" and "hat" can't be told apart, let alone "mama" and "papa."

Alexander Graham Bell, inventor of the telephone and a teacher of the deaf, concocted a famous "trap sentence" to illustrate the ambiguities of lipreading. He would say, "It rate ferry aren't hadn't four that reason high knit donned co." A deaf lipreader might think Bell had said, "It rained very hard and for that reason I did not go."

Lipreading is not so much a skill as it is a knack, and it's best cultivated at a very young age. A tiny child's linguistic world is a simple one: two adults—mother and father—and perhaps a sibling or two. Their words and gestures become familiar and predictable. As the child grows older, that world expands, but it is still largely a small, familiar, and comfortable one of friends and school, of other children's mothers and teachers.

In the 1940s and 1950s, when I was growing up, almost all American elementary school teachers were women. American women, whose culture does not train them to suppress their feelings, are much easier for most deaf children and deaf adults to understand than are most American men, who have grown up in a society that values a poker face. For a lipreader, expressiveness must substitute for inflections and differences in emphasis that shade the meanings of spoken words. A cock of the head or slightly raised eyebrows, for example, can mean a question is being asked. Brows that reach the roof can indicate disbelief. A single raised eyebrow implies skepticism or contempt. The sentence "It was you who said it" can have three meanings, depending on whether the stress is on "was," "you," or "said." A nod of the head, a jut of the jaw may be the only clues that a word is being emphasized.

Even region and nationality make a difference in expressiveness. In adulthood I have found that New Yorkers, who speak as fast as they can while moving their lips as little as possible, are exceptionally difficult to understand, while American Southerners of both sexes seem warmly expressive, relaxed, and easy to lipread. Foreigners, who tend to form words deep in the mouth and throat rather than with the lips, can be frustrating targets for the American lipreader. English-speaking French and Italians are relatively easy to understand, once the lipreader is accustomed to their particular accents, for their body language is eloquent and helps plug the holes of understanding.

Even for a child, the major component of lipreading is guesswork. It's often said that only 30 to 40 percent of lipreading is actual "reading" of each word; the rest is "context guessing" to fill in the gaps between the words that are actually understood. Did the teacher say "hat" or "cat"? The last three words of her sentence—"Put the hat on your head"—tells the deaf child that the teacher can't be talking about a cat.

Early on, a deaf youngster learns that much of what people say in everyday situations can be predicted. Most of the time, for example, a dime-store salesclerk will say, "That'll be X dollars and XX cents" (a sum confirmable with a quick glance at the cash-register readout) and "Thank you. Have a nice day."

In this way lipreading is like filling in the blanks in a crossword puzzle. It's far easier for the lipreader to understand someone if he already knows the subject of the conversation, for he can anticipate the words used to discuss it. If the subject is, for example, the Chicago Bears, a deaf pro football enthusiast will unconsciously be wating for proper names such as "Ditka" or ever "Wojciechowski"—words he'd never understand in any other context.

Proper names are the lipreader's bane. We never catch names during introductions; "John Smith" is easy enough, but "Matilda Grosvenor" will fly right past. As an adult, I learned long ago, I can in certain situations simply ask for the other person's business card and at an opportune time sneak a look at it. Often, however, I must fall back on an old deaf person's gambit I learned as a youngster: if I am introduced to a stranger, then must repeat the introduction to someone else, I mumble inaudibly and allow those concerned to smile thinly and perform the introductions themselves.

Conversations among more than three or

four people are nearly impossible for even highly skilled lipreaders to follow. It takes a few moments to catch the rhythm and sense of one person's words; by the time we're in the groove, someone else will be speaking. Often we never catch up, falling further and further behind as our minds slowly make sense of what we're seeing. Once in a while the light of understanding will shine upon us long after the talk has passed to another topic, and we'll drop into the conversation a comment or observation based on the old subject. It might be witty—even brilliant—but it will land with all the grace of a gooney bird on an asphalt runway. Fortunately, early on my friends learned to be amusedly tolerant of these appalling non sequiturs.

For lipreaders, one-on-one conversations are much easier—easiest if our interlocutors are at all familiar to us. It will take anywhere from a few moments to a few days to become accustomed to a stranger's speech, depending on how limber and expressive the stranger's mouth and face are. I can consistently understand somewhat fewer than 50 percent of the people I meet for the first time, but familiarity will raise the level of understanding to 75 to 80 percent. Perhaps

10 percent of the people I come across will always be impossible to lipread.

There is, fortunately, a good deal of humor in the lipreader's predicament. Since I was a child, some of my misunderstandings have brought gales of laughter I couldn't help joining in with. A few have become oft-told family anecdotes. Some years ago, for example, during the flu season, I sat one afternoon in the living room reading a book while suffering from a typhoon in the bowels. Suddenly and prodigiously I broke wind. My elder son, Colin, then five years old, dashed in wide-eyed from the kitchen and inquired, "What's that big loud noise?"

Mystified, I arose from the couch, peered out the window, and said, "*What* pig outdoors?"

My son stared at me dumbfoundedly. What *pig*?

Go ahead, look in the mirror and watch your lips: to a lipreader "What's that big loud noise?" looks exactly like "What's that pig outdoors?"

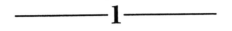

Only connect! . . . Live in fragments no longer. Only connect, and the beast and the monk, robbed of the isolation that is life to either, will die.
— E. M. FORSTER, *Howards End*

When we newspapermen turn the last page of our lives, we are praised at the wake and forgotten after the grave. Our achievements, after all, are as transitory as the events we chronicle. What will we have produced that will last? In my case, perhaps this book about my deafness.

One of the reasons I have written it is to help fill a void. There isn't a large body of literature about the deaf by the deaf. A good deal more has been produced by educators of the deaf, parents of the deaf, and offspring of the deaf. Much of it is valuable but tinged by second-handedness. Other than modest and brief testimonials, chiefly published by small specialty presses and marketed within the deaf community, little has been written by the deaf themselves. Their handicap has kept most—especially those born deaf—from achieving the necessary command of English.

Another impetus for this book comes from an extraordinary series of events that occurred in March 1988 in Washington, D.C. It began with the proclamation that "deaf people are not ready to function in a hearing world." What a stupid thing for the chairwoman of the board of a university for the deaf to say! When the news arrived at the Chicago *Sun-Times*, where I am an editor and critic, I was astonished. But soon my surprise gave way to gratification, some amusement, and not a little dismay.

I have long been accustomed to the paternalism of all too many hearing educators toward the deaf. Until then it had seemed a subtle and silent paternalism, not an overt one. But when Jane Spilman brought it to the surface, she set in motion a tidal wave that is still lapping on the shores of deafness around the world.

She made the remark in attempting to justify the appointment of Elisabeth Ann Zinser as the new president of Gallaudet University, the nation's only liberal arts institution for

2

the deaf. Spilman and her board of directors had chosen Zinser, the only one of the three finalists for the position who was not deaf, despite months of urging from both deaf and hearing people that the new president share the students' deafness. By all accounts, Zinser, who was then vice president of academic affairs at the University of North Carolina at Greensboro, was a competent and even brilliant administrator. But she had no experience with the deaf and, like Spilman, could not speak American Sign Language, the required method of communication at Gallaudet.

To the students and most of the faculty, the appointment—never mind Spilman's incredible remark—was incendiary. It was as if a white had been chosen president of a college for blacks because they were too incompetent to produce one themselves. But, as with blacks, there are successful deaf scientists, lawyers, journalists, professors (at hearing colleges as well), deans, dentists, and doctors. Why not a college president? Especially at their own university?

The ensuing events were like a replay of the campus demonstrations of the 1960s. The Gallaudet students, galvanized into uniting against the ignorance, thoughtlessness, and paternalism that for so long had been their lot, took to the streets. They waved placards, blocked traffic, and chanted slogans in sign language. The nation's news media, weary of a long and dull presidential primary campaign, descended on the campus. Jesse Jackson, that canny campaigner and old civil rights worker, was photographed clasping hands in victory with student marchers.

At first I was appalled. After all, I considered myself the unlikeliest person to sympathize with campus upheaval of any kind. I am middle-aged and vividly remember the abortive college sit-ins and takeovers of the 1960s and 1970s. Today I'm paying thousands of dollars a year in tuition for my own collegian. I had expected I would have little accord with anything that disrupted the expensive process of higher learning.

But within a day or two I began marching with the Gallaudet students in spirit if not in person. After all, right was on their— *our*—side. So, it turned out, was might. The students' storming of their Bastille was no noisy and ineffectual campus rebellion, but a true revolution in which an oppressed but bright and well-organized group succeeded in seizing its rightful share of power.

To my considerable delight, the board of directors, under enormous pressure, caved in to all the student and faculty demands: that there be no reprisals against protesters, that Spilman resign, and that a majority of the board be constituted of the hearing-impaired. (Only four of its members were deaf, and all had voted against Zinser's appointment.) They also gave the presidency to one of the deaf finalists they had passed over: Irving King Jordan, Jr., the popular dean of the Gallaudet college of arts and sciences. The board immediately elected a deaf chairman, Philip Bravin, a New York business executive, and began restructuring itself to give hearing-impaired members a majority.

And so the good guys won. The victory seems to have been a heaven-sent opportunity, too. It may unite the hearing-impaired of America in facing a larger task: to prove to an indifferent (and sometimes hostile) hearing world that we are capable of taking our rightful places in society. Everywhere.

It won't be an easy job. Because the rhetoric during the Gallaudet demonstrations sounded so much like that of two decades ago, some journalists and commentators misunderstood what had happened. One ultraconservative syndicated columnist, for example, likened the uprising to separatist Black Power tactics of the 1970s. Superficially that's true. If deaf people sometimes appear self-segregated, working and socializing chiefly among themselves, most (like American blacks) have had little choice in a world that has tended to ignore and even reject them. But the deaf have not echoed the militaristic rhetoric and implicit violence of the Black Panthers, nor have they rejected the values of the hearing world, as the black militants loudly repudiated those of white America. The deaf have hardly been perceived as a threat to the stability of the hearing world. Apart from their brief flurry of revolutionary grandiloquence at Gallaudet, they have quietly asked only that their community be accepted as a proud, legitimate member of the plurality of cultures that makes up the United States.

Other journalists displayed abysmal ignorance in their eyewitness descriptions of the demonstrations. I was highly amused when reporters used the terms "silent" and "soundless" when writing of the marches. For the deaf tend to be noisy people, both vocally and in their actions. Even if most speak in sign, many use speech as well.

And I was chagrined when it became apparent that journalists covering the Gallau-det story tended to write as if all deaf people were members of the self-contained "deaf culture," relying exclusively on sign lan-guage. Homogenizing the deaf in this way is like assuming all black Americans to be Democrats.

We are not all the same. Though I have been totally deaf for forty-six of my forty-nine years, I am a member of a minority within a minority: I am what is called an "oralist." That is, I depend wholly on spo-ken language and lipreading, however im-perfect they might be, to help me live and work in a hearing world. I do not know sign language at all.

For centuries there has been a gulf be-tween the few speaking deaf and the many signing deaf, and not simply because we can-not, for the most part, communicate with one another. For a long time, especially in recent years, we—and our teachers—have quarreled over whether deaf children should be taught speech or sign.

Deafness frequently begins in the womb, the advocates of sign often point out. The normal fetus hears its mother's crooning, and during the first two years after birth the child constantly soaks up sound. Missing all this, deaf-born children almost never catch up. If they learn to speak at all, it's usually in an almost unintelligible pidgin. Only sign language, the argument continues, can give deaf infants an easily learned, natural, and efficient way to communicate. It's undeniable that sign can be rich, dramatic, and powerful. The National Theater of the Deaf and such compelling plays and movies as *Children of a Lesser God* are proof that those who master sign can be as poetic as the Irish. But sign, counter the oralists, is not the best way to communicate with a hearing world that employs a wholly different language. Without speech, a deaf person will always be an outsider.

It's often pointed out that those like me —the deaf who master English and speak intelligibly—almost always have lost their hearing after having learned language. And their ability to lipread varies widely.

Nowadays many deaf children learn a compromise called "total communication," the act of speaking and signing English at the same time, often with the use of residual hearing if the child has any. In theory it's a sensible idea, say oralist critics, but in practice the simultaneity slows down both speech and sign and distracts the listener, hearing or deaf, who does not know sign. And for most children speech tends to be overshadowed by sign, for the latter is far easier to learn. Likewise, those who favor American Sign Language, which has a syntax of its own utterly unlike English, complain that total communication forces its users to sign in English word order, an almost incomprehensible pidgin version of ASL.

With such wrangling about methods of communication, it's hardly surprising that popular books on deafness tend to be intense and one-sided. Almost all in the last twenty years have favored sign, for until a sea change in the education of the deaf that occurred in the 1960s, most of the history of deafness in America was the history of oralism, the unrelenting and largely unsuccessful attempt to teach *all* the deaf to speak and read lips without relying on sign language.

Though I was reared in the oral method, this book is not an attempt to discredit one side of the issue and advocate another. The abilities of the hearing-impaired to communicate by one method or another differ vastly, as do the degrees of their hearing loss and the ways in which they cope with it. The loss may be total, severe, modest, or slight.

It may have occurred in childhood or in adulthood. Some born without hearing also suffer from other handicaps, such as cerebral palsy.

Some hearing-impaired people, both speaking and signing, are bright, vital, aggressive personalities for whom no challenge is too great; some are dull, timid, and withdrawn, and prefer the path of least resistance. Most of the hearing-impaired, like the hearing, fall between those extremes. Sign language is best for some, lipreading and speech for others, and a combination of the two the most sensible compromise for many.

In this book I intend simply to tell my own story. If at times I sound like an advocate for oralism, it is because many deaf people who speak and read lips believe that they and their accomplishments have been minimized as unrepresentative and therefore unimportant by those who champion membership in the community of the signing deaf. To ignore the advantages of speech and lipreading for the few is as foolish as belittling the benefits of sign language for the many.

Still, I have no axes to grind, although from time to time I have taken issue with professional advice (often from oralist educators) given to my parents and me through the years. My experience may help some parents decide on the best course of action for their hearing-impaired children. It also may offer insight to educators—especially those sensitive enough to recognize that studies, statistics, and laboratory testing do not reveal the whole potential of an individual deaf child and that parents' insights and wishes are not to be dismissed.

Most important, this volume is intended to help the hearing public understand something of what life is like for those who cannot hear. Deaf people share certain similarities with blind people, for each has suffered the loss of a sense. Our afflictions, however, are not the same. The consequences are profoundly different. Blindness is a handicap of mobility, deafness one of communication. Terrible as is loss of vision, it does not distance the blind from the sighted the way loss of hearing separates the deaf from the normal. Deafness opens up a huge social chasm between sufferers and nonsufferers. In the hearing world, deaf people tend to be solitary and ignored if they are lucky, lonely and rejected if they are not. That is why Samuel Johnson called deafness "the most desperate of human calamities."

Can deafness be "conquered"? Nonsense. That's a sentimental notion beloved by writers of inspirational literature. But, like a wolf at the edge of the forest, it can be held at bay.

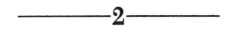

"**Y**ou just keeled over in the car beside me," Mother remembers. That morning someone at the Fort Lauderdale Naval Air Station, where Dad was assigned, had declared I looked "peaked." I had had a recent throat infection. There was no other warning of illness during that first week of January 1944. I was not quite three and a half years old.

When we arrived at home, Mother put me to bed, where I lay by turns somnolent and delirious, sometimes in a coma, as my temperature soared. For three days Mother and Dad called in Navy doctors, who thumped my chest, peered into my orifices, shook their heads in bafflement, and departed.

Then, on the fourth day, as the fever hovered at 104 degrees, Mother and Dad phoned Dr. Robert Blessing, a physician from Evanston, Illinois, who had retired to Florida but had been called back into harness by World War II. After a brief examination he swept me up in his arms and drove me to Broward County Hospital. His initial diagnosis was "purulent meningitis." Not for several days did he make an official diagnosis, and even then he wasn't certain of it.

Meningitis is a bacterial infection of the meninges, the membranes that envelop the brain and the upper part of the spinal cord. The symptoms are high fever, headache, stiff neck, and vomiting, and they are often preceded by a respiratory illness or sore throat. The patient usually progresses through irritability, confusion, drowsiness, stupor, and coma. Dehydration and shock sometimes follow. Today the fatality rate for acute meningitis is less than 10 percent when it is recognized early and treated with antibiotics. In 1944, however, only sulfa drugs were available. They often helped, but as is the case today, much depended on how soon treatment was started. Fatalities were common, and those who survived tended to suffer long-lasting physical consequences— such as deafness.

Furthermore, as late as the 1940s it was sometimes difficult to distinguish between meningitis and its close cousin, encephalitis, a *viral* inflammation. Most cases of encephalitis occur as a complication of viral infections such as measles, chicken pox, rubella, and smallpox vaccinations. Many of its symptoms are similar to those of meningitis. The symptoms I had were high fever, a stiff neck, and painful swelling and paralysis in my left knee and left arm. I was put into isolation and pumped full of fluids, Seconal, and sulfa. Dr. Blessing ordered a spinal tap and hot packs placed around my neck, back, left arm, and left leg.

The next day the spinal fluid findings indeed suggested a purulent meningitis. But the clinical symptoms, Dr. Blessing thought, bespoke encephalitis. What's more, he wrote on my chart, the painful muscles in my paralyzed left arm and leg could indicate a particularly dangerous cousin of encephalitis—polio. He kept me on sulfa, but because he still suspected meningitis, he asked the Navy to see if it could locate a rare anti-influenzal serum. It couldn't.

I was so acutely ill that my survival hung in the balance. But on the third day in the hospital, the seventh since onset, Dr. Blessing thought I looked a bit better. My neck was less painful and the knee swelling had subsided somewhat. I was lucid again. But the doctor was still uncertain what it all meant. "I cannot say there is no paralysis or paresis," he wrote on the chart, "but cannot say there is. . . . Are we going to settle down to a Still's disease [rheumatoid arthritis]?" The improvement continued through the fourth and fifth days, and I began to move my left leg and arm.

Then, on the sixth day, Dr. Blessing entered this ominous sentence on the chart: "There is some question of acuteness of hearing." Shortly thereafter he called in my parents and broke the shattering news to them: "Your child is deaf."

My subsequent recovery was rapid, and on the ninth day of hospitalization I was sent home. I was not able to walk, but Dr. Blessing considered the problem a "pseudoparalysis" that often accompanied encephalitis and would disappear in time. His diagnosis at discharge: influenzal encephalitis.

It this indeed what it was? A neurologist at the U.S. Army Hospital at Coral Gables maintained not long afterward that I must have been suffering from meningitis, because deafness is a classic consequence of that disease. Recently, however, my family physician reviewed the records and speculated that I had taken a "one-two punch," suffering from *both* meningitis and encephalitis— and that it was the meningitis that had

16

caused the deafness, for the long period of high fever it brought had destroyed my auditory nerves.

Upon learning that I had lost my hearing, my parents had, of course, suffered the classic reaction of emotional devastation. "I was in a trance," Mother says. "I felt the usual 'It isn't fair. It can't happen to one of my children.' But we were relieved that you were alive."

For many parents, the verdict of deafness is like a death sentence for their child. How, they ask distraughtly, will their youngster be able to grow up to be a functioning member of society instead of being "deaf and dumb," a representative of a less-than-human species to be pitied and scorned if not simply ignored? Even today some parents all but go into mourning over what appears to be the loss of their dreams.

Others are overcome by feelings of guilt and helplessness. Was there something they did not do that they should have done? Or something they did that they should not have done? For a long time Mother believed that if she had called Dr. Blessing earlier instead of the ineffectual Navy doctors, the siege of meningitis might not have been so severe and

I would not have lost my hearing. It probably would have made no difference.

Aside from guilt complexes, the literature of deafness contains many heart-wrenching stories of parents who refused to accept their child's loss of hearing, persisting in the futile faith that the sense would return or, if it did not, that somehow the child would look and behave exactly like a normal one. This, however, was the single ray of hope for my parents during my early days at home after the illness. Many well-meaning people, including doctors, said that as I learned to walk again, my hearing probably would return.

Dr. Blessing thought there was a slim chance, but he was not otherwise sanguine. His report of a checkup two months after my discharge reads: "Plays around office *well*, is good, and cooperative. He is obviously deaf but is very quick at anticipating requests. The family thinks he can read lips. I doubt this. I cannot demonstrate any neurological abnormality. There is no ataxia. Personality changes are certainly minimal now. . . . I think 'Hank' has made a very complete recovery with the exception of deafness and consider him fortunate. I think he must be under the continued observation of an otologist to evaluate the extent of nerve deafness, plan his teaching and care."

Today, once parents have recovered from the shock of discovery that their child is deaf, they are greeted by a wide range of public and private resources. One choice for their child might be the mainstream of a local public school. Another might be a well-appointed state school for the deaf, or a more luxurious private day or residential institution. Any might offer oralism, sign, or "total communication." (Total communication currently is the most common method, especially in public schools; American Sign Language is gaining strength in both public and residential schools; and oralism is nearly moribund and survives mostly at a few private institutions for the deaf.)

In Fort Lauderdale, Florida, during that war year of 1944, few resources were available to the parents of a newly deafened toddler. Oralism was the sole officially approved method of teaching the deaf. But only in a few large cities did public schools offer programs for the deaf, almost always segregating them from the hearing. Elsewhere institutionalization was the norm—in a meagerly funded state school if the child was unlucky, in a wealthy private school if he was lucky.

19

My parents had to make do with what they had. And, as it turned out, their greatest resource was their robust self-reliance.

Looking back from the perspective of more than forty years, I believe that if any parents ever were well suited to cope with a newly deafened child, mine were. Both Mother and Dad are intelligent, cultured, and tough-minded, with an eye for what we today call "maximizing possibilities." They are proud and resolute and profoundly skeptical of educators who, solely on the basis of a brief round of testing, offer diagnoses and prognoses with absolute certainty.

My father, Manown Kisor (his first name, his mother's maiden name, is Irish), is descended from the sturdy German-Irish stock of the steel country around Pittsburgh. He inherited the Irish way with words—he is a splendid writer and a storyteller of rich humor—as well as a taciturn stubbornness often associated with emigrants from Prussia. As a schoolboy he displayed considerable brilliance and attended the Virginia Military Institute for a year. Then he won an appointment to the U.S. Naval Academy and graduated in 1934. During the Depression the impoverished peacetime Navy could offer active duty to only half of its Annapolis graduates, and Dad was not chosen because of nearsightedness that had developed while he was at the academy. He entered civilian life, taking a junior executive job with Montgomery Ward in New York City, where he met Judith Merrell Du Bois, my mother, in 1935.

Mother comes from a mixture of French Huguenots and English who settled in northeastern Pennsylvania during the last years of the eighteenth century. Her paternal grandfather was a politician and diplomat, a consul in Germany and later Colombia; hermaternal grandfather, a physician. After World War I her father helped build a railroad across Persia for the first Shah of Iran and later rose high in the U.S. intelligence community. During the 1920s he took his family with him to the Middle East and Europe, where Mother learned to cope each day with the unfamiliar and the extraordinary, developing a headstrong independence not altogether uncommon among young women of her age and station at that time. (Her stubbornness, in fact, matched Dad's, and the trait eventually would stand me in good stead.) Thanks to her family's foreign sojourns, she was fluent in French and German and had a smattering of Polish and Farsi. When the Du Boises returned to the United States in the early 1930s, she attended Chevy Chase, a junior college near Washington, then Scudder Secretarial School in Manhattan. The first job she found in those early years of the Depression was at the Bank Street School in New York City, typing manuscripts and operating the elevator, much to the horror of her aristocratic father. Before long, however, she found a more "suitable" secretarial position at Minnesota Mining & Manufacturing, where she was working when she and Dad met on a blind date.

After they married, Mother and Dad set up housekeeping in Flushing, New York, where my brother, Manown Jr., nicknamed Buck, was born in 1936. Later the family moved to New Jersey, first to Wortendyke and then to Midland Park, where they were living when I arrived on August 17, 1940, at a maternity home in nearby Ridgewood. It was a perfectly normal birth and I a perfectly normal infant, with all my senses as well as fingers and toes. When I was a year old we moved to Ho-Ho-Kus, a tiny town just down the pike from Ridgewood.

From the first, it seems, I was linguistically precocious. When I was two years old and Dad had entered the wartime Navy as a Supply Corps lieutenant stationed first in Jacksonville, then at Fort Lauderdale, Mother drove us down to Florida. All the way, she recalls, I sang "The Eyes of Texas Are Upon You"—every single word. I also had an extensive vocabulary and spoke clearly and fluently, without baby talk. Mother and Dad thought I had some musical talent as well. But now, as that awful winter of 1943–44 waned into spring, the first question to emerge was: How much hearing loss did I have and how best to deal with it? The second: I already could speak, and speak well; how best to train me to retain my speech?

My maternal grandparents, who happened to be wintering in Florida when disaster struck, took Buck under their wing so that Mother and Dad could devote their time to me. When I returned home from the hospital, my grandparents and two elderly cousins, both schoolteachers in New Rochelle, New York, immediately urged that Mother and Dad show me pictures in magazines, sounding out the names of the objects so that I would not lose my concept of language. That was futile; the hearing loss was too great.

A more immediate problem was teaching

me to walk again. Not only did the pseudoparalysis linger but the disease had also burned out another function of my inner ears—I had lost my sense of balance. Dad took over this job, pulling me up from a sitting to a standing position.

I learned to walk again just as a baby does: a few tentative steps, then a frantic series of lurches, punctuated by tumbles and pratfalls. So awkward was my slowly recovering left side that I adopted a marked lean to port, like a drunken sailor. Within a year, however, I had straightened up and ambulated along normally. So long as I had a horizon to fix my eyes upon, I could keep my balance. My eyes were beginning to compensate for my lost ears.

And during those first months of regaining my toddling skills, I began to pick up the art of reading lips, in crude monkey-see, monkey-do fashion. For some time, however, my prowess was only rudimentary. Except for reading on my parents' lips the names of concrete objects that could be shown to me, such as "apple" and "milk," I could understand very little. Abstractions were quite beyond me, and when I could not understand them my frustration would spill over into tantrums, often with a lot of head banging. "When you wanted chewing gum," Mother remembers, "I couldn't explain that there wasn't any because the air station commissary store had run out. I had to drive you out to the air station to show you the empty shelves."

Worse, I began to stop talking. At first my voice departed; I'd move my lips normally, but no sound came from them. Then I stopped doing even that and withdrew into utter silence.

Growing ever more concerned, Mother and Dad took me to specialists in New York and Philadelphia. Most thought I had some residual hearing, because I often seemed responsive to hearing tests. What I actually did was anticipate their cues with a little elementary lipreading and a lot of guesswork. "You were so bright and alert that you fooled people," Mother recalls.

All the experts, however, declared that there was little or no hope that I could ever regain my hearing. They recommended that my parents look for teachers of the deaf and begin planning for my education. One specialist in Philadelphia curtly suggested that Mother and Dad "accept the fact" that I was deaf and send me away to school. My parents—bless them for it!—refused to entertain the notion. They began to look around for alternatives.

The family faced other concerns, for Dad had volunteered for sea duty. The Navy ordered him from Fort Lauderdale to Hampton Roads, Virginia, to join the aircraft carrier *Randolph*, nearing completion in the shipyards. There was a severe housing shortage in and around that bustling Navy base, and the family home in Ho-Ho-Kus had already been rented.

So, as did many service families during World War II, we threw ourselves on the mercy of relatives. With our two parakeets, we bundled into the car and drove to Dad's parents' home in Monessen, Pennsylvania, and then to Dad's elder sister's house in Milton, Pennsylvania.

There we stayed for six weeks while Buck remained home with the mumps and I attended a neighborhood preschool. (Interestingly, Mother remembers that I "got along well" with the other three-and four-year-olds in that group, though I didn't speak much, if at all. I was rapidly expanding my lipreading horizons, she recalls, and probably could understand much of my playmates' simple speech.) After we wore out our welcome in

Milton, we drove to Mother's family's farm in Hallstead, Pennsylvania.

In July, Dad at last found housing in Portsmouth, Virginia, and the family moved there to be with him. A bit later, while visiting her parents in Washington, D.C., Mother stopped at the Alexander Graham Bell Association for the Deaf, a national service organization for the deaf and hard-of-hearing. There she picked up a copy of the *Volta Review*, the organization's monthly magazine, and came across this advertisement:

Deaf Children Trained only by
Parents with Help of the

Parent-Child Training Institute
during its few years of operation are now working successfully in their home town public hearing schools, 2nd, 3rd and 6th grades.

Your Child Is Just as Capable
This Institute makes no profit.
Constant advertising is not possible.

Save This Address

3 Charles, Montgomery 7, Ala.
Tel. 3-6130

Spotting this ad was a great stroke of luck for Mother and Dad, for it introduced them to a "miracle worker" we'll forever remember as "Miss Mirrielees."

Those who sheltered under her wing still call her Miss Mirrielees, with the same respectful emphasis on "Miss" that an Englishman might apply to "Sir" when addressing a brigadier knighted for heroic service to his country. Like Johnny Appleseed, Doris Irene Mirrielees was an eccentric original—an itinerant bearer of hope whose passion and devotion deeply touched every child and parent she encountered. Her unconventional ideas and techniques affected my life profoundly.

When she answered Mother's letter of inquiry that day in 1944, Miss Mirrielees had been a private live-in tutor for perhaps half a dozen families with deaf children. She had developed and refined what was then and in some ways still is a revolutionary philosophy. Mother and Dad responded to it immediately, for it addressed their concerns about me as did no other method they had yet encountered. Miss Mirrielees believed that the educational establishment had failed the deaf. Inefficient, uncaring teaching methods had produced large numbers of semiliterate adults fit only for menial tasks. The underlying cause, she felt, was that most educators, especially those in the ubiquitous residential schools for the deaf, equated deafness with retardation. Of their charges they expected little and received less. Residential schools, therefore, seemed to Miss Mirrielees nothing more than holding tanks for the hopeless. In her view they taught deaf youngsters, not the difficult arts of coping with a hearing world on its own terms, but only the primitive skills necessary for a sheltered, low-income existence.

Miss Mirrielees was passionately certain that all deaf children could enjoy lives as full and productive as those of their hearing peers, if only they could acquire the gift of language—the *whole* gift, not a small part of it—as soon as possible. To do so, she argued, very young deaf children, like their hearing brothers and sisters, needed the security and love of life at home. Only in such a "normal" environment, she believed, could a deaf child's intellect blossom under her theories of teaching.

An old idea was the kernel of her new

method. In a memoir privately published in 1952, Miss Mirrielees told how, as an undergraduate at Chicago Normal School at the turn of the century, she had learned a technique called "Plan Work." In it, older, more advanced deaf pupils used a common experience as a base for learning new language. From the simple idea of a milkman arriving at a house with bottles of milk, for instance, the pupils would learn—as the teacher acted out the roles in a heavy pantomime—how milk helped them to grow, how refrigerators cooled the milk, and so on. New ideas about milk would be added to their general knowledge. To show how things are related was the aim of this method; it taught how language worked to express abstractions.

At that time most schools for the deaf taught only rudimentary English—simple nouns and verbs of the "Apple is food. I eat apple" variety. A deaf child did well to learn fifty-two single words—one a week—by the end of his first year. This, Miss Mirrielees argued, was absurd. Teaching single words, or two words at a time, was teaching deaf children not language but simple actions and responses, just as a dog learns to fetch a thrown stick and earn a pat on the head. Rather, deaf children ought to learn that words stood for abstractions as well as objects and actions. They should learn not only that a thing is called a "rose," she wrote, but also that it "is a flower, that it smells sweet, that it is beautiful in color and form, that it grows from a tiny bud, helped by the sunshine and rain, that it should be treasured and cultivated because it brings happiness and pleasure to everyone who sees it."

Miss Mirrielees tirelessly argued that deaf children could catch up to, and keep up with, their hearing peers in language development —if they were given the right means. But how? The process of language learning begins before birth; the normal fetus hears and responds to sounds from outside. Conversely, it's well past birth when most parents of deaf babies learn the devastating truth, and by then their children are not just one but several steps behind their peers, who have been exposed to the stimuli of sound ever since and perhaps before emerging into the world.

The catching-up process should begin immediately, Miss Mirrielees maintained, with parents placing their faces in the baby's line of vision, so that the child could associate the movements of their lips with objects and actions and begin learning the rudiments of lipreading. But Miss Mirrielees knew that lipreading was too exhausting a method of taking in large amounts of information over long periods of time. The answer, instead, lay in the printed symbol of the spoken word.

In short, she believed in teaching deaf children to read almost as soon as they could focus their eyes. And not just in single words but in entire phrases and sentences with the full rhythm and content of spoken English, in the same way hearing children learned language. The difference was that deaf children would "hear" with their eyes, not their ears—and would do so *before* they learned to speak.

Miss Mirrielees believed that deaf children could become familiar with words, and their proper order, by actually handling them— by choosing them from among other words and placing them in sentence form. When she was a child, Miss Mirrielees recalled in her memoir, her teachers "had passed out small cardboard boxes to the 'good' children of the class as a special treat when they were excused from Friday afternoon lessons. In such boxes one would find a paragraph of print pasted to a piece of cardboard, and the individual words of the paragraph pasted singly on cardboard slips. It was considered a reward for her goodness that she was allowed to put the words of the paragraph together, using the paragraph pasted on the large cardboard as her model."

Much later she read in the biography of a famous author (whom she never identified) that he had improved his work by "taking paragraphs from great literature, cutting the individual words apart, and then trying to reassemble the paragraphs." It was a quantum leap backward from a professional writer whose aim was lapidary prose to a deaf child who hadn't even a crude concept of language, but Miss Mirrielees made the jump. If the writer could perceive the rhythms and subtleties of English syntax by assembling and reassembling single words on paper, she reasoned, the deaf child could also learn its rudiments, and more, with the same method. Thus what she called "Chart Work" was born out of the old idea called "Plan Work."

Chart Work began with Miss Mirrielees creating an event in the child's life, such as taking the youngster to a farm. She'd make sure that the child not only saw a cow, for instance, but also saw that it ate hay and produced milk, which was collected in a bucket. When they returned home, she would draw pictures on a blackboard of the cow, the hay, and the bucket of milk. As she drew the objects and acted out their relationships, she would also say their names, making sure the child watched her lips. Then she would write the name of each object under its picture, saying the name as she did so.

But she did not stop there. This was not merely "cow," "hay," and "milk." "The cow," she would say slowly, "eats hay and gives milk," acting out the verbs as she wrote them along with their nouns on the blackboard. She would repeat the words, pointing to their pictorial and written representations on the blackboard, until the child had made the connections among the three kinds of symbols—pictorial, written, and spoken.

Later Miss Mirrielees would progress from blackboard to large paper charts on a wooden stand, using a set of large rubber type to stamp the words under pictures either drawn or cut out from newspapers and magazines. Each chart carried a complete story made up of several sentences. When the chart was done, the child's mother and father would copy it onto cardboard, cutting out each word on rectangular strips, then assembling the whole into proper order in a pile of strips bound together with a rubber band: "The," "cow," "eats," "hay," "and," "gives," "milk."

The goal was for the child to learn not merely what the shapes—drawn, printed, and spoken—stood for but also their proper arrangement. As time went on, the child learned to place each cardboard rectangle containing a word on the table in correct order, mimicking that on the chart. This was how Miss Mirrielees taught English syntax. The meanings and order of concrete nouns and verbs were easy, but the abstract parts of speech—articles and conjunctions—took longer to learn. This, however, is exactly the way hearing children experience language. Only in this case the form of the symbols was different.

It should be pointed out that Miss Mirrielees did not emphasize teaching all deaf children to speak the words at the same time they learned their visual shapes. Nor did she immediately place a great deal of significance on the pupil's watching the movements of the teacher's mouth as she wrote or printed words on a chart. The time for learning these skills depended on the age of the pupil, whether the deafness was from birth or from disease or accident after the rudiments of spoken language had been learned, and whether the loss of hearing was complete or only partial (and thus could be alleviated with hearing aids).

Speech and lipreading, Miss Mirrielees believed, were to be emphasized only after the thorough assimilation of printed language had given these skills a solid foundation, a better chance to succeed. Once the notion was firmly planted in a child's mind that printed thoughts could be strung together into a necklace of ideas, then the arts of conveying and understanding them on the lips could be engaged.

What was most controversial about the Mirrielees Method was its reliance on the parents of deaf children as its vehicle. Miss Mirrielees saw her major task not as a teacher of the deaf but as an instructor of parents, who, she believed, rightfully possessed the keys to their children's vaults of language, speech, and lipreading. In the 1940s, authorities in the education of the deaf warned parents that shouldering such a grinding responsibility was impractical and even dangerous.

Miss Mirrielees knew home teaching would be a wearying task. Regular hours must be devoted to it. The deaf child must be taken somewhere nearly every day for experiences upon which to build lessons. Charts and materials must be prepared. All this must be done in addition to the normal tasks of parenthood.

But, she argued, her method was neither difficult to understand nor hard to put into practice. She saw no reason why a mother could not teach her own child, although educators warned against it (she dismissed these warnings as "professional self-aggrandizement and egotism"). Backwoods pioneers, she said, had educated their children at home. Ambitious modern parents of hearing children consciously encouraged their learning. And unconsciously, parents were always teaching their youngsters.

By the early 1940s Miss Mirrielees had begun distilling her experience into manuals that she left with each family to follow after her departure for the next one. Some of these mimeographed, hand-bound manuals still exist. Designed to fill every possible inch of a long, legal-sized sheet for reasons of economy, they are laboriously typed in tight single spaces, with the narrowest of margins. Hand-corrected typographical errors abound. Mechanically, these manuals are difficult to read, although they are fluidly and clearly written for the most unsophisticated of housewives, the profession of most women of the day.

Soon Miss Mirrielees began selling these manuals by mail to parents with whom she could not work in person. She had been advertising her services in the *Volta Review*, the most prominent publication in the field, and it was one of these advertisements my mother had seen.

At that time, during the summer of 1944, we had moved into "Skunk Hollow," the dilapidated, makeshift quarters in Portsmouth for the families of Navy officers. I had no idea where we were or why we had moved there; no one knew how to tell me. But while Dad worked to help prepare the *Randolph* for her sea trials, Mother settled down with Miss Mirrielees' first lessons. Nearly every day, following the teacher's dictum to provide me with memorable experiences, Mother (with Dad's help evenings and on weekends) would take me for walks in the countryside, and then, while what I had seen on my trips was fresh in my imagination, make charts and hang them up for me to look at. Soon these charts of crayoned pictures and rubber-stamped sentences became not merely schoolroom tools to me but a kind of Book of Life that no other child I knew was lucky enough to own, and I was proud of them.

Even though I couldn't speak, I still had a child's knack for making friends easily. Some of those friends quickly joined our little "classes"—as many as eight or ten at a time. For them it was like a preschool, and they were enthralled by the preparation and presentation of the charts of my outings. As I learned to read, so did they. Big Bird would have been proud.

This experience of learning along with hearing children was an early form of "mainstreaming"—the philosophy, still controversial today, of educating deaf children as much as possible with hearing classmates of the same age. Its immediate result was that though I might be deaf, for a remarkably long time I never felt "different" from my peers. I didn't know any better, and neither did they.

At some point a few months after Mother and Dad had begun the Mirrielees lessons, I experienced an epiphany. Though I had stopped talking, the concept of speech had never quite left my subconscious, and as I learned to read from the charts, somehow I made the connection between printed and spoken language. Dad remembers that the breakthrough was a jubilant moment very much like the occasion when Helen Keller exultantly learned her first word—"water" —as Annie Sullivan pumped it over her hands. It would make a better story if I or my parents could recall the exact word I spoke, but I'm afraid we've all forgotten.

Whatever it was, it loosed the floodgates of language. As speech returned to me, with it came the knack for lipreading. In fact, I thought *everybody* read lips. When I talked to people, I'd grasp their faces and turn them toward me so that they could see mine. Evidently I assumed everyone was deaf like me. Eventually I did learn that they weren't, but by then I'd decided, with all the off-center wisdom of a small child, that deafness was a minor, if interesting, human characteristic, like freckles, blond hair, double-jointedness, or the ability to teeter along the top of a board fence.

Each morning for two hours, sometimes more, I'd sit at a little table and assemble sentences, mimicking the charts. Little by little my reading vocabulary grew. And after that first breakthrough, so did my speech. Some sounds were easy, others more difficult. The consonant "m," for instance, was a snap. Mother would press her lips together, flare her nostrils, and engage her larynx—*mmmmmmmmmmm*—while holding my little hand first to her throat so that I could feel the vibrations there, then to her nose for the same reason. *Mmmmmmmmmmm.* Easy. Mustn't let too much air out the nose, though. Hold back a little. There. You've got it, Hank! Ooh!

Oooooooooooo. A little harder but not too much. It's easy enough to pooch out the lips and switch on the voice box, but that's only the half of it. *Ohhhhhhooo.* Too much like a low rumble in the back of the throat. The vibrations of the larynx need to be focused in the front part of the mouth, with the help of the tongue as well as the lips. *Ooooooooo.* See, Hank? Feel it right here, on both sides of your mouth? That's it!

To this day, however, the sibilant "s" gives me fits. Producing it properly requires the tongue to be placed just so, behind and perhaps a little lower than the juncture of upper and lower teeth. The tongue must be shaped and tensed in a certain fashion, too, and the difference between the right way and the wrong way is very small. How does a teacher get all this across to a four-year-old

42

who hasn't the slightest idea of the anatomic structure of the maxillary cavity? Not easily. *Thsthsthsthsth.* Nonononono, says Mother, with a slight shake of the head. Try again. *Sthssthssthssth.* That's better. C'mon, once more. *Sssthssssss.* A huge smile. Good enough for government work.

Mother had to be my jailer as well as teacher. Four-and five-year-olds have the attention spans of shrews; ten minutes after beginning a two-hour session, I'd demand to be let out to play with my friends, who with normal childhood capriciousness sometimes tired quickly of our "play school." Some days degenerated into a two-hour contest of wills. I was adamant, but Mother was immovable. Until every last lesson of the day had been learned, she wouldn't release me from battleground to playground.

During these go-rounds I learned a trick that infuriated my parents. When I'd been naughty and Mother or Dad was laying down the law, I'd shut my eyes tight so I wouldn't "hear" the scolding. If I couldn't see it, I must have reasoned, it wasn't happening. Does a tree falling in the forest make a sound if no one is around? It certainly does, and I quickly learned why in the form of a sharp thwack across the seat of the pants. A few more swats cured me of the habit. Just the same, lipreading a chiding is much harder than it sounds. Can *you* look someone in the eye while he gives you hell?

On October 9, 1944, the *Randolph* was commissioned, and Dad went to sea. While the carrier steamed to the Caribbean on its shakedown cruise, Buck, Mother, and I drove to Ho-Ho-Kus for the duration. It was not a good time for Mother. She resented Dad's volunteering for sea duty and leaving her with all the responsibility for my training. Worse, all the way up to Ho-Ho-Kus I cried and screamed, as four-year-olds will on long auto trips, while my brother gasped between attacks of asthma. Fortunately, Mother recalls, the old Ford we owned had only one door that would open—the driver's—and she didn't have to worry about one of us tumbling out onto the highway. A trooper stopped her for speeding, but when Buck informed him at the top of his voice, "My dad has gone to sea!" she was let off with a warning.

Before the *Randolph* sailed to join the Pacific fleet, Dad came home to Ho-Ho-Kus on a brief leave. There he spent hours teaching me to ride a bicycle, a process that, because of my damaged sense of balance, took a long time and was more nerve-racking than the usual bumps, scrapes, and bruises of a normal childhood. As I've said, so long as I had a definite horizon to focus upon, I could walk normally. Pumping pedals, keeping handlebars straight, and staying upright, however, was an infinitely more complex undertaking. But I learned. Soon I was riding on the sidewalk, then in the street. As I wobbled out into traffic with my playmates, Mother's and Dad's hearts welled up into their throats.

Miss Mirrielees had urged them to allow me to live as independent and normal a life as possible, and they stuck to this wisdom, though other parents would phone them to announce indignantly, "I almost hit Hank with my car this morning!" It was Dad's belief that they hadn't come within a country mile of doing so but just wanted to express their outrage that a handicapped child wasn't being sheltered from life's everyday perils. (To this day "Caution Deaf Child" traffic signs make me wince. The parents who demand them on their streets mean well, but I can't help wondering what sort of self-image, let alone self-reliance, such signs create in the youngsters they are intended to protect.)

In Ho-Ho-Kus, Mother continued to labor with me, using Miss Mirrielees' methods —not just Chart Work but the conventional speech and lipreading drills she advocated after the groundwork had been laid. "Bee, even, Jean, whee, mean, green," I'd say, attempting to sharpen the long "e" sound into one that would please Mother. Our task no longer was one of crude shaping but more delicate polishing. By early 1945 my speech had become quite intelligible, though nobody would mistake my breathy monotone and foggy articulation for the voice and speech of a normal hearing child. And I had a gift for lipreading. So long as my interlocutor faced me, I could communicate with almost anyone who dealt with children of my age.

My world broadened. Before becoming deaf I had understood, even as a toddler, that the country where I lived was fighting a faraway place called Japan, where people looked different from us. And I had understood that Dad wore a blue uniform because he was helping fight the yellow-skinned, squinty-eyed, buck-toothed caricatures I saw in propaganda posters everywhere on Navy bases. Otherwise I was in a soundless limbo about the rest of the world. Only after

I had acquired enough language to uncover the facts through lipreading and print did I learn about Hitler and the Nazis. One of my earliest and most vivid memories is of a sunny spring day in 1945. While playing in a horse trough on my grandparents' farm in Pennsylvania, I looked up to see Mother dashing down the hill from the farmhouse, tears of joy streaming down her face. "The Germans are finished!" she cried. "The Germans are finished!" I was rooted to the spot, for even as a four-and-a-half-year-old I knew exactly what Mother's words meant: the fighting in the Pacific would be over soon, too, and Dad would come home.

That fall, Mother drove me to the local public school in Ho-Ho-Kus to enroll me in kindergarten. I was eager to join my hearing playmates, but would the teachers accept me? I knew and cared nothing about such matters as I dashed gaily into the large kindergarten room. Two of my friends, off in a corner, beckoned me over to help them build a house of blocks.

Earlier, Mother had taken me to meet the principal. I had an advantage, Mother recalls, in that the principal and his teachers knew little or nothing about the deaf. In that small public school there was no teacher of the deaf; indeed, there were no other deaf pupils in the community. "Nobody had any preconceived ideas what deaf children could do or could not do," Mother says. "We all just expected you to do almost everything."

My being able to read his lips and talk with him was important enough, but what evidently persuaded the principal to take a risk on an unknown deaf child was my ability to read. Today, thanks to *Sesame Street* and parental ambition, reading is a commonplace achievement for preschoolers. But in the 1940s it was still a rare accomplishment. I was reading far ahead of my age group, so much so that Mother thinks I was better known in the little community as the five-year-old who could read than as the town's only deaf child. The principal, visibly impressed, told Mother that though the school had never had a deaf pupil, he was most willing to give me a try on a year-by-year basis. There was no argument from the teachers either, for the same reason.

The Mirrielees Method had done its work well. Not only had it enabled me to catch up to my contemporaries in the ability to use language, it even had given me a head start.

Just once, when I was six or seven years old, did I stand in Miss Mirrielees' presence. Little memory remains of the brief encounter: just a foggy image of a tall, thin, benevolent wraith in bobby sox and white tennis shoes, the whole topped with a bun of gray hair. She had been traveling, and had stopped in at our home in Ho-Ho-Kus to see how her pupil-once-removed was faring.

I was not the only deaf child who benefited from the Mirrielees Method. As far as I have been able to determine, her teachings set more than a score of deaf children on the road to successful and fulfilling lives among the hearing. Why, you may ask, was the Mirrielees Method not widely accepted by the deaf educational establishment of the time? The answer is complex. For one thing, she dealt in heresies. She promoted the renegade notion that parents could teach their deaf children not only to read but also to speak and read lips. Moreover, she was far ahead of her time in contending that very young children could learn to read. (Only recently have researchers confirmed that infants as young as fourteen months of age can indeed distinguish among shapes of letters and words and understand their meaning.)

Perhaps worst of all, she possessed few professional credentials. She had earned no college degree and offered no mountains of research data to support her contentions. All she could muster was anecdotal evidence about the successful lives of a few deaf children.

In her memoir (in which she refers to herself as "the Teacher"), she tells how "the grandmother of a youngster whose mother had been a correspondence pupil of the Teacher took the child to visit the [Bell Association] headquarters' offices [in Washington, D.C.]. The child already, following his pre-school home training, had been successfully entered in public school. Much admiration was expressed by the incumbents of the Authorities' office for the child's accomplishments. Then came the inevitable question, 'And where did he go to school?' When the answer disclosed that his mother had been his preschool teacher with the help of the Teacher's correspondence course, the interview was ended on a strong note of disapproval."

Most likely I was that child. My maternal grandmother, who supported Mother wholeheartedly in her use of the Mirrielees Method, lived in Washington, and I often stayed with her and my grandfather in the summers. I dimly recall having visited the Bell headquarters with my grandmother, though of course I would have been unaware of any disapproval. Nonetheless, many years later in the 1970s when I was a successful journalist, I got a taste of it. In Washington on business, I dropped by the Bell Association and met its president. When he asked how I had been taught speech and lipreading, my answer brought forth an expression of surprise, consternation, and skepticism.

"But you are *adventitiously* deaf," he said. "That must have made all the difference."

Possibly having learned language before becoming deaf did mean a great deal to my later success with speech and lipreading. But I have no residual hearing, another factor frequently cited as being largely responsible for whatever oral success a deaf child might have. Neither, for the most part, do most of the former Mirrielees Method graduates I have been able to locate in recent years. There was, we are all certain, considerable merit to Miss Mirrielees' theories.

In the course of researching this book I not only met Ann Percy, the daughter of the novelist Walker Percy and herself a Louisiana State University graduate and

successful bookstore proprietor, but also cor-
responded with Lamar Cason, a former Mirrielees pupil who is currently a chemist in
Tennessee. He married Helen Estus, yet
another successful Mirrielees product. The
Casons are both deaf, as is Ann Percy, and
they give much credit to the Mirrielees Meth-
Method for the successful rearing of their
own deaf children. While Ann has remained
a champion of oralism, however, the Casons
long ago added sign language to their rep-
ertoire. Sign was a method of communication of which Miss Mirrielees, who was in
many ways a product of her oralist times,
disapproved highly.

Yet the teaching of sign and the Mirrielees
Method have a great deal in common.
Though their vehicles could not be more different, their aims are nonetheless identical:
to give deaf children the priceless diamond
of language at the earliest possible moment.
I can't speak for others, but I believe that
the Mirrielees Method not only gave me a
good chance at a normal life among the hearing but also laid the groundwork for my
profession as a journalist. It gave me a deep
love of language for its own sake.

Perhaps a researcher someday will discover a set of Miss Mirrielees' dusty old

mimeographed manuals, study their ideas, and put them to the test in a rigorous academic setting—the test she always sought but never could obtain for her work. It's hard to dispute the idea that American Sign Language most likely is the quicker and easier way to communicate for those born deaf or those who are deafened before acquiring language. But those who advocate "signed English" over the more "natural" American Sign Language might find a valuable adjunct to their philosophy in the Mirrielees Method.

And for certain fortunate children—luckier in their home situation and perhaps in their native intelligence than others—the learning of printed and spoken English as their first natural language might give them an important advantage: an early mastery of the primary tongue of the hearing world.

—————4—————

From ages five to thirteen—that lovely, unhurried span between innocence and adolescence when time and growth almost stand
still—my life was for the most part no different from that of an ordinary American
youngster. So little happened in my childhood that did not also occur in those of my
hearing contemporaries that, to all intents
and purposes, I was just another kid on the
block. That was my impression then and it
is my impression now.

As I remember it, my childhood was the
kind of American sentimentality Norman
Rockwell painted in *The Saturday Evening
Post:* idylls of dogs and barbershops, skin-
ned knees and bloody noses, baseball in the
spring and football in the fall, Thanksgiv-
ings with turkey and Christmases with
ham. I made friends and skylarked and
fought with them. One day we swore blood
oaths of mutual support and the next declared our perpetual enmity. The following

week, of course, the grand alliances were restored.

One hot summer day, in classic six-year-old entrepreneurial fashion a friend and I set up a lemonade stand on the parkway in front of my house and did a modest business with the few passersby. Suddenly more customers than we could handle dropped in on us in the form of the entire local volunteer fire department, returning from a brush blaze nearby. The mayor was also the fire chief, and after he and his men drained our few jugs, he munificently pressed a five-dollar bill into my hand—more money than I had ever seen in my life.

That winter I scared the bejesus out of Mother and Dad when, sledding down the long steep hill that ran by our house, I somehow flipped over in a rut and zoomed upside down into the curb behind a parked car, my Flexible Flyer emerging riderless from under the front bumper just like a Laurel and Hardy movie gag. Dad immediately took me to the family physician, Dr. Tomkins, a tall, graying, mustachioed general practitioner who strikingly resembled Boris Karloff and carried himself with the same solemn, almost funereal gravity. The doctor assayed the damage, pronounced it a mild concussion, and told me from now on to watch where I was going. Later on Dr. Tomkins would not only lance an abscess in my ear but also yank my tonsils and adenoids, a common if wholly unnecessary procedure that ought to have cemented the solidarity of the entire generation who had to suffer it. He had thought the surgery might improve my hearing, but his efforts were to no avail.

And, as do seven-year-olds everywhere, I fell in love with my second-grade teacher, mooning dreamily over her lush, dimpled blondness every time she passed my desk, my heart leaping when she tousled my hair. She was a ringer for Jane Powell, a dewy-eyed film star of the 1940s. I was very put out that summer vacation arrived and school was out before she realized that she, too, was crazy about me.

My childhood was so stereotypically "normal" because my parents planned it that way: they wanted me to be just like any other American child of my time and place. This was "mainstreaming" before anyone had conceived the term.

Chance and location also had a good deal to do with the success of my mainstreaming. The open-minded little community of Ho-Ho-Kus was partly a small town and partly a bedroom suburb of New York City, almost entirely middle-class and full of young war veterans beginning their families. We were all white, mostly Protestant but with a smattering of Jews and Catholics, and upwardly mobile. I think that to most of the good citizens of that community, a deaf child was simply a mildly interesting phenomenon, to be remarked upon approvingly but forgotten so long as the child's welfare seemed in competent hands.

Certainly there were differences among us children, but they were few and, to me, seemed perfectly ordinary. A couple of times a week, for example, my Catholic friends had catechism class after school. I had speech class. By 1947 Mother had taken me beyond the Mirrielees Method, which was designed for very young children. So long as one listened carefully, I was understandable, and so long as I "listened" with my eyes, so were the familiar people around me. But Mother and Dad believed my speech could be better: my enunciation more precise, my voice more pleasant.

My speech, they thought, had reached a point where improvement was beyond their ability. They also wanted me to broaden my lipreading horizons beyond our circle of family and friends, to learn to lipread strangers. So they set out to find a specialist. They found one almost two hours from Ho-Ho-Kus via a drive to the George Washington Bridge, then the subway to Brooklyn. "You'd talk and a voice pattern would appear on a screen," Mother recalls. "I don't think you benefited much." The "screen" probably was an early oscilloscope, on which the specialist attempted to quantify differences between my speech and that of a hearing child. Electronic technology would remain too crude to be of much benefit to me for more than thirty years to come.

On one of those outings we stopped in Manhattan to visit the Lord&Taylor women's apparel store on Fifth Avenue. In true small-boy fashion, I turned in one direction while Mother, engrossed in her shopping, went another way. After a time she looked down and discovered that I was not with her. Frantically she called and called, her heart in her mouth. Naturally I did not respond. What are the consequences when a deaf child disappears in a crowded, cavernous department store on a busy New York street? Exactly what happens when a hearing child gets lost. She found me a few aisles away, intently admiring a display of naked mannequins.

In any event, the twice-a-week, two-hours-each-way journey became too wearying. Its sole benefit seems to have been that Mother learned to read lips while talking with me on the subway. The trains' rattle and roar drowned my small voice, and she'd watch my lips carefully as I chattered on to her about the doings of the day. (Some of my best friends learned to read lips, too. Silently we'd gossip and giggle across the classroom, much to the puzzled annoyance of our teachers, who had no idea that lip-reading was contagious.)

Mother and Dad cast about for another private teacher. Luckily, they found Jean Swart in Tenafly, half an hour from Ho-Ho-Kus. She was a gifted oral teacher of deaf children and also taught lipreading to adults. For two years, twice a week after school, Mother would drive me to Tenafly for my hour-long lessons.

I don't remember them as being in the least bit onerous, for Mrs. Swart, a born ringmaster, knew how to win and keep a child's attention. She'd ask me about my adventures since our last session. While I bubbled on about building forts and catching frogs, she'd listen carefully to my speech and observe how well I read her lips, making unobtrusive mental notes about sounds and words that needed work. All the while she'd ask intelligent questions—intelligent to a seven-year-old, that is—to keep me going.

She'd notice, for instance, that my "p" sounds were much too explosive and often accompanied by a coarse spray. My "Peter Piper picked a peck of peppers" sounded like a machine gun in a monsoon. As a toddler I had learned to produce the sound in classic, exaggerated deaf-child fashion: building up air pressure behind tightly closed lips a few inches from a lighted candle, then releasing the air in a sudden and loud "pah!"

Mrs. Swart used the same technique, but in reverse. "Can you say 'pah!' to the candle but not blow it out?" she asked. My first attempts failed, but soon I got the hang of reining in the air pressure. Little by little I learned to produce gentler, drier "p"s and other plosive consonants, such as "t" and "k."

We were all happy with Mrs. Swart, who thought my progress satisfactory in every way. She thought my potential such that she asked Mother and Dad whether they wanted me to speak with a New Jersey accent or a cosmopolitan one. They chose the latter, and to this day I believe that some of my pronunciations—such as "been" with a long "e," in the Continental way, instead of the American "bin"—come from her influence.

Mrs. Swart also advised Mother and Dad to let me stay in public school with my hearing contemporaries while having me take private lessons in speech and lipreading. Throughout my childhood, however, Mother believed in exploring every possible avenue for my development. Late in 1947 she took me to the famous Lexington School for the Deaf in New York City for testing. It was a residential oral school, but also had day pupils as well as an experimental course for parents who wanted to help in their children's education.

After we had visited a few times, one of the more astute Lexington teachers took my parents aside and told them privately that I did not belong there, that my speech was already so fluid and understandable that she was afraid it might slip if I was taught among other deaf children of less developed oral skills. Thanks to my interaction with hearing children, I was speaking with normal cadence and syntax, whereas the other deaf youngsters at Lexington still spoke woodenly, each word plodding after the one before in the same flat, dull tone. The teacher thought I'd be better off where I was, in a public school with hearing children. She was one of the few special education teachers I have ever encountered who willingly gave up a potential pupil, who frankly admitted that the child's accomplishments were beyond her powers to improve.

On one of those jaunts to New York City I acquired my first and only hearing aid. Because I was so responsive to visual cues too subtle for adults to perceive, Mother and Dad thought I might have some usable residual hearing. Possibly I did, but if so, it was difficult to measure. The crude auditory equipment of the day could pump out only raw volume at varying pitches. Low-frequency vibrations, when loud enough, set my eardrums to thrumming in response, and I could feel a tickling in my ears. Feeling the vibrations of high-powered auditory testing is not hearing. A seven-year-old child, however, doesn't know the difference, and my "I can hear it! I can hear it!" gave everyone—including me—the wrong impression.

As a result, I wore an experimental, specially built aid designed by technicians at the New York Hearing Society. It was a large black brick of Bakelite accompanied by a heavy rectangular dry cell battery, the whole contained in a brown canvas harness to be donned and buttoned like a vest. It was meant to be worn under a shirt, only the cord and large ear button being visible. In the beginning, however, I preferred to wear it outside my clothes. I thought I looked like a paratrooper with grenades clipped to his battle dress, and I wanted everyone to admire my quasi-military equipage.

At the very least, thought Mother and Dad, the aid would allow me to hear doorbells, automobile horns, and train whistles. For two years I wore the apparatus and willingly, even eagerly, suffered the consequences of the hearing aids of the time. They were not only heavy and clumsy but also had a tendency to emit horrible squeals of feedback whenever the ear mold worked loose —and it often did, because I was a physically active child even while sitting. Two or three times a day at school, my classmates would stiffen in their seats, turn to me, wave their hands, and shout, "Your hearing aid! Your hearing aid!" There must have been a special corollary of Murphy's Law that dealt with powerful hearing aids in school assemblies, churches, and other quiet public places. The adults may have been horrified and even pained, but we youngsters all considered the sudden squeals an amusing diversion.

Nonetheless, as time went on my enthusiasm for the aid waned. I came to realize I really wasn't hearing anything, and by age nine I asked Mother and Dad if I could stop wearing it. The episodes of feedback were no longer a novelty but had become a tiresome annoyance to me and to everyone else. Moreover, the harness had grown heavy and cumbersome. By then Mother and Dad had also realized its limitations. To them the aid's only usefulness was as a visible signal to strangers that its wearer was deaf, and that was hardly sufficient reason to keep me wearing it. Quietly they assented to my request. The aid went into a dresser drawer and was eventually forgotten.

The hearing aid was the centerpiece of one of the rare episodes of my childhood in which my handicap caused me genuine pain at the hands of another child. I had gone to a drugstore with Mother, and while she picked up a prescription I lingered in front of the candy counter. A slightly older boy, one of the town bullies, walked up behind me and spoke to me. Of course, I did not hear him, and when I failed to answer he took a roundhouse swing with an open hand and struck me hard on the ear that held the hearing-aid button. The blow drove the ear mold into the ear, cutting the skin. The wound was superficial, but it was painful and bled heavily. The boy ran, and Mother took me home squalling. When my brother heard of the incident, he immediately wanted to go after the bully, but Mother stopped him. One of Buck's friends, however, was equally furious and not so restrained. He sought out the boy and administered a thorough drubbing. Rough justice was done and the incident forgotten.

There were so few such instances of cruelty that once the initial surprise and outrage wore off, they were easily dismissed. I was fairly big and strong for my age, as well as an athlete competent enough to be one of the first chosen for games, and that was sufficient deterrent to most contemporaries with a mean streak. Older bullies also knew that Buck and his friends could be hard-nosed enforcers. So the peace was kept.

Of course children taunt one another, but in those early years my deafness never seemed to be a reason for my friends to do so. Mother and Dad waited for such a day, but it never came. One afternoon when I came home crying, Mother thought, with her heart sinking, "Now it's happened. Somebody's made fun of Hank because he's deaf." Indeed, I had been singled out for a physical peculiarity. But not the one Mother thought. The males in my family tend to be stocky and blocky physical types, even as children, and a playmate had teased me because of my "stubby fingers."

In Ho-Ho-Kus there was just one other untoward incident that related to my deafness, and I did not learn about it until decades later, when I interviewed Mother and Dad in preparation for this book. Our immediate neighbors were the local Episcopalian rector, his wife, and their daughter Claudia, who was my age. When we were about six, Claudia and I naturally became playmates. One day Claudia's mother persuaded herself that my deafness was giving her daughter what she called a "quirk." Just what that was none of us recall, but she announced to my mother that Claudia would no longer be allowed to play with me. Claudia's father saw no harm in his daughter having a deaf child as a playmate, but his wife ruled the roost. I don't recall ever being told explicitly not to play with the little girl; in any case, I had a million other friends, for, as Mother and Dad recall, I was "a happy, outgoing child with a great sense of humor."

Not long after my eighth birthday Dad's employer, Montgomery Ward & Co., transferred him from the New York corporate offices to its headquarters in Chicago. On December 19, 1948, we drove up Lake Shore Drive, stormy gray Lake Michigan on the right and Chicago's snaggletoothed skyline on the left, to our new home in Evanston, a suburb abutting the north side of the city.

Moving to a new city is ordinarily a wrenching experience for a child, even a hearing one. Until they're settled in with new friends in new surroundings, most children feel like displaced persons. To me the relocation was an adventure. The constant moving about of a Navy family was not long in our past, and I was still too young to have put down firm roots. The prospect of new playmates in a new town, far from being daunting, was exciting.

Dad had bought our modest, though comfortable new house without Mother having seen it. It was the best one we could afford in the well-to-do area around Orrington

School, the only elementary school in Evanston that had its own teacher for the deaf.

Evanston was more than ten times the size of Ho-Ho-Kus. Its school district was composed of eight or nine separate elementary schools and two junior highs, and had a small but distinct special education program. The school officials and teachers of this sophisticated suburb did not possess the wholly open minds of those in the tiny Ho-Ho-Kus schoolhouse, but they displayed a certain flexibility. So long as a pupil performed well academically and socialized acceptably with his peers, they would not interfere with his parents' wishes.

And they weren't above concocting an amiable bureaucratic fiction when it suited the situation. A few years later, when confronted by my parents' request that I go to the same North Side junior high school as my hearing neighbors—the junior high that had the program for the deaf lay far in the southern part of the suburb—the officials would reclassify me as "hard-of-hearing," although I was obviously deaf as a post. The northern school had a teacher who specialized in the hard-of-hearing, so why not essay a small experiment?

But that lay in the future, and the present

would lead to some disappointment. After we celebrated Christmas in our new home, I was taken to Orrington and immediately placed in the mainstream. I studied all subjects except one with my hearing classmates. Each day, while the rest went to music class, I'd go to speech and lipreading with the teacher for the hard-of-hearing.

It was not long, however, before I came home with a sheet of paper the teacher had given me. On one side was a list of hobbies for the hearing and on the other a list of hobbies for the deaf. I don't recall what the hobbies were—in fact, I don't remember the episode at all. But Mother and Dad went through the roof. They would have no truck with the assumption that deaf children automatically cannot do certain things. Only when I had tried them and failed could they be set aside as impossibilities. Mother and Dad insisted that I be removed from the hard-of-hearing class while they sought private speech and lipreading lessons elsewhere.

At the same time, the regular third-grade teacher informed Mother and Dad that, despite my prowess in reading—I tested two years ahead of my age group—she was going to put me back at grade level with the rest of my classmates, reading the same books they did. At some point in my education, she told them, I would have to read at grade level, and it might as well begin in third grade. Forty years later, in an age in which teachers strive to identify and nurture special gifts and talents among their charges, such an action seems astonishingly short-sighted. In the 1940s, however, less adventurous teachers often attempted to reduce their pupils to the lowest common denominator. It was easier to teach that way. So much for the vaunted Orrington School.

All the same, I don't think that teacher's benightedness harmed my reading development. Though I read more difficult schoolbooks than most of my classmates, I was not a frail genius whose intellectual flowering had to be gently tended, but just a moderately bright kid who had had an early leg up. By age nine, anyway, I had begun reading a great deal outside school, and continued to do so. I found my intellectual treasure trove was not in the adult classics (as so many celebrated novelists seem to have done at very young ages) but in newspapers and magazines. Each evening Dad brought home the Chicago *Daily News*, and after the funnies and the Cubs (in those days, as it is today, it was difficult to distinguish between them), I'd read the front-page stories. The Washington and foreign news, I am sure, was well above my level of understanding. The crime stories, however, entranced me, much to Mother's disgust. I had had no idea that people could kill each other in such colorful ways and for such strange reasons.

Mother was too wise to forbid me to read anything, but she must have had her doubts when she walked into the living room to find me on the sofa engrossed in *The Ladies' Home Journal*. I had no interest in the service articles about clothes and food, but I loved the "Can This Marriage Be Saved?" column. The vagaries of human behavior toward the opposite sex were wonderful entertainment, although I doubt I understood the bedroom problems that the column explored with great delicacy and euphemism. At age nine I still didn't know a thing about the sexual act, nor would I have believed it had I been told.

At this time I also began reading *Time, Life,* and especially *The Saturday Evening Post*, whose pages I would devour as soon as the mailman arrived with it. I fell in love with Clarence Budington Kelland's droll stories about the adventures of a salesman

71

named Botts and his Earthworm Tractor Company. This was not literature but slick sentimental entertainment. Of course, I didn't and couldn't make the distinction; to me, a story was a story, whether fiction or nonfiction, and the joy was in the telling. At that time, perhaps, the seed of the future journalist was planted.

If that school year of 1948–49 was a wasted one, as Mother and Dad still believe, I did make some good friends during it. I still had that sunny good humor which helped wary hearing children to accept my deafness despite my odd, breathy speech and the necessity of facing me when they spoke to me. One of them was in a similar situation. Sam Williamson was not another deaf child but a fellow newcomer to Evanston, having arrived from New Haven the month before when his father, a professor of economics, moved from Yale to Northwestern University. New kids tend to gravitate toward one another for mutual protection, and we became fast friends for life. Sam is now a professor of economics at Miami University in Ohio, and his older brother Bill, who became a chum of Buck, is also an economist, at the University of Illinois. (Economics seems to be a hereditary disease in that family.) Sam was the first "best friend" I ever had, and his mother, Arline, a gentle and loving surrogate mama. The Williamsons' house was close to Orrington School, and twice a week Arline made lunch for Sam and me while Mother was off at Great Lakes Naval Hospital being a Gray Lady, a kind of grown-up candy striper.

Meanwhile, Mother and Dad had found private speech lessons for me at the Institute for Language Disorders at Northwestern University, a few blocks from our home. For several months I had lessons with an elderly couple famous for their work with deaf babies in England. The Ewings—later Sir Alexander and Lady Irene—and I got along very well, and they improved my speech markedly. They even, quite inadvertently, gave me my first instruction in the difference between British and American English.

While testing my vocabulary by showing me pictures of objects and asking me to name them, the Ewings displayed a drawing of a familiar item of feminine appurtenance. "Pocketbook," I said confidently. "No, Hank, that's a *purse*," they replied. "Pocketbook!" I insisted. To me and my friends, a purse was a small bag with a clasp for holding coins. It could be carried inside a woman's pocketbook. "Purse," they countered. *"Pocketbook!"* I replied vehemently. What strange ideas these British people had! Meanwhile, the Ewings shook their heads and smiled as they wrote in their notebooks. Doubtless the deaf American child had confused a purse with a small paperbound novel and did not want to admit his error.

Darn right I didn't. I knew they didn't believe me, and I seethed. When they brought me out to Mother after the session, I immediately grabbed her pocketbook. "What's this?" I demanded. "It's a pocketbook, isn't it?" "Yes, honey," she replied indulgently. I was triumphant. I doubt that the Ewings heard the exchange, for they neither apologized to me nor acknowledged Mother's confirmation. To me this was not a trivial matter, a simple bruising of a child's pride. Inconsequential and even irrelevant as it may seem, it was the first of many disagreements I would have with authorities in the field of deaf education. (Not that I was always right, as I was in this case!)

My experience with the Ewings led to an episode in which one matter was settled and another raised. Mother recalls that our immediate neighbors insisted, as did many people, that I must have retained some hearing because I seemed, in their words, "so normal and responsive." So did the Ewings, who mistook my skill at anticipating and guessing their statements for evidence that I must have a great deal of residual hearing. They decided that my hearing should be extensively tested.

And so it was, by the head of the institute at Northwestern himself. Helmer Myklebust was a renowned authority in the field of deaf education. For six solid hours one spring day, he subjected me to a battery of auditory tests, carefully designed to ensure that there would be no visual cues. A few years before, I had mistaken sympathetic vibrations of the eardrum for genuine hearing. I had also inadvertently fooled testers when they turned up the dials and asked, seemingly out of my line of sight, if I could hear the tone—and I replied, "No." I simply had (and still have) excellent peripheral vision, and had guessed correctly when I saw the movements of the tester's lips far to my left. What else would they say but "Do you hear anything?" I had no intention of deceiving anybody—I just thought I was being a nice, cooperative little boy.

Finally, late in the afternoon, as ants of impatience gnawed away at me, Myklebust admitted the truth. I had no measurable hearing. I was deaf. Totally and completely. Not slightly, partially, or profoundly, or hard-of-hearing, or any of the other degrees of and euphemisms for hearing loss. At last the matter was settled.

But Myklebust, who had made his name as a psychologist of the deaf, also declared that I was "tense" and "hostile," and needed some psychological therapy. Dad, who had taken me to Northwestern and had stayed there for the entire six-hour session, lost his temper. "Of course the kid is tense!" he said. "Any normal child would be tense if he'd been asked all day to do something he can't do!" And with that he swept me out of the building. I would not return to it for more than a decade.

On separate levels both Dad and Myklebust probably were right. A six-hour battery of tests is bound to try a child's patience and affect the results. Dad knew that outside the psychologist's laboratory I functioned well, in all ways a happy nine-year-old child growing up in a limitless world. Had Myklebust been out in the field for weeks, observing my normal everyday interactions with hearing adults and children, perhaps he would have come to different conclusions, ones that acknowledged that I perhaps displayed a larger potential for success in the hearing world than most deaf children. It's not always easy for social scientists to recognize exceptions to the rules they formulate, especially if the data for those rules come entirely from testing in the laboratory. In those situations, "counseling" might do more harm than good. In 1949, I am certain, it might have proven more a hindrance than a help. A few years later, perhaps not. For a seed of truth was buried in Myklebust's findings, a seed that eventually would sprout and take root.

In any event, Mother and Dad by this time had no doubt that they had chosen the right path for me. I was doing well at Orrington School, keeping abreast of, if not a little ahead of, most of my classmates in all subjects—even, of all things, drama—and had built up a large new circle of friends. An emblematic memory of the time comes from an October day in 1951 when I walked out of school to see a knot of boys gabbling excitedly around a classmate with a portable radio. One of my friends peeled away from the group and dashed over to me. He joyfully punched my shoulder. "The Giants won the pennant!" he cried. "Bobby Thomson hit a homer in the last of the ninth!" I have never been certain whether Steve wanted to be sure his deaf friend knew what had happened or whether he simply was sharing momentous news with the nearest warm body. I like to think it was the latter: that I was just another kid in the schoolyard.

Certainly I was doing everything the other youngsters were, even taking lessons on musical instruments. My parents thought musical instruction might benefit my speech, even if they weren't quite certain exactly how. They didn't force me into it, as so many reluctant hearing children are; they simply asked if I was interested, and I eagerly said yes, because I had the normal eleven-year-old's enthusiasm for new experiences.

Mother and Dad paid the small fee for private after-school lessons with the school's instrumental teacher, who manfully tried to guide me in what must have been several extraordinarily painful—for him—sessions with the trumpet. I understood the broad notion of a musical note: it was a certain frequency of vibration. I had no idea, however, how to produce it, let alone when. I never could synchronize the vibrations of my lips on the mouthpiece with the fingering of the valves. Occasionally, quite by accident, I'd hit upon some semblance of a note, and the teacher would praise me for doing so. But I never could repeat the note.

Stubbornly I kept on, session after session, the teacher sitting beside me sweating as profusely as I was, marking the proper valve fingering on the sheet music before me and gritting his teeth over the sounds I produced. To call those sounds off-key was probably to flatter them. Finally I admitted defeat. "Do you think I should keep on doing this?" I asked the teacher in frustration. "I don't want to." Immediately he smiled, sighed with relief, and gently took the trumpet from my hands. For weeks he must have been waiting for me to say those words.

At the time I didn't think my lack of success all that unusual. Some of my friends had also tried, and failed, with musical instruments. Big deal. So we weren't cut out for that sort of thing. Musical illiteracy was simply another characteristic we shared. They were *tone* deaf, and I was *deaf* deaf. If there was a difference, the consequences were the same.

In other ways we shared success. Most of

the boys in my fifth-grade class joined the Evanston YMCA, which had an excellent afternoon program for boys as well as a summer camp in Michigan. The Y staff was as open-minded as anyone could be about deaf children in their programs, and they were also willing, at Mother and Dad's behest, to allow me to seek my own level. Two or three times a week, we fifth-graders would take a bus downtown after school for swimming lessons.

In the summers some of us took the bus to Camp Echo, which the Y operated in the woods near Fremont, Michigan. Though some of the boys were filled with the usual ten-year-old's horror at being separated from his parents for the first time, I wasn't. Those summer visits with my grandparents had accustomed me to being away from home. Like a grizzled old veteran lecturing a bunch of recruits, I airily told my cabin mates that their homesickness wouldn't last, that camp was terrific and c'mon, let's have some fun.

At camp and at the Y my friend Sam and I became quite proficient in the pool and were asked to join the Y's age-group team, he as a backstroker and I as a free-styler. In the beginning, because I couldn't hear the starting gun, I swam only on relays. But since I was a stronger swimmer than most —partly because I had entered puberty a bit earlier than my friends and was putting on muscle—Dad and the coach thought I might also excel in individual events if only I could get a good start. They tried placing me in the lane closest to the starter so that I could feel the vibrations of his pistol. The results were inconsistent. In a small, closed-in pool, I could sometimes feel on my skin the crack of the .22 pistol if it was a particularly loud one. Most starter's guns, however, didn't produce vibrations strong enough to register on me.

So I learned to keep one eye on the left hand of the swimmer to my right. As soon as it moved, off I'd go. Of course, there was a noticeable delay in my start, but with time and practice Dad and the coach helped me get the lapse down to two-tenths of a second or so. Today, when winning margins are often measured in hundredths of a second, that might not seem like much help. But in the schoolboy competition of the 1950s, it was plenty. Soon I stood out from the crowd as a swimmer and began to win my share of medals in regional age-group competitions.

It wasn't long before my rivals learned that they could make me false-start by twitching their hands as we got into the "set" position. On a false start, the starter would fire his pistol a second and a third time to halt the swimmers before they'd got more than a few yards down the pool. Whenever that happened, one of my teammates had to jump into the pool to grab me before I worked up a head of steam. Three false starts and a swimmer was disqualified. The officials, however, quickly sized up the situation and announced that anyone who tried to make me false-start would himself be banished from the event.

In the typical American family unit of the 1940s and 1950s, the mother was the dominant figure at home while the father went off to work, and the Kisor household was no different. Mother took on the major responsibility for my speech and lipreading, and for persuading dubious educators to take a chance with a deaf child. We were close and still are, perhaps more so than other mothers and sons, because she invested so much time, energy, and emotion in the upbringing of her deaf son.

Mother is of a type well known, and much disliked, by educators of the deaf: one who, they say, refuses to accept the reality that her child is deaf and will not allow her child to accept his deafness. This sort of mother, they contend, is aggressive, demanding, pushy, certain of her position, contemptuous of others, and absolutely unreasonable. Not only will her child fail to live up to her absurdly high expectations; the emotional stresses that ensue are almost certain to cause personality disorders.

That this sometimes happens I have no doubt; I have met more than one troubled deaf adult who is a product of this scenario. But it did not occur at our house. Mother wisely did all her pushing and shoving and wrangling behind the scenes, keeping her son utterly unaware of it. Rather than force me to do things that I could not do, she simply created a large space in which I could try my luck, and if my efforts did not work, go on to something else. She allowed me to be independent. She gave me room to learn how to balance success against failure and accept the results with equanimity.

She accepted the reality that I could not hear. What she refused to accept was the concept of deafness held by most of the educators she met: that a deaf child should not be too ambitious, because the world will not allow him to achieve his goals, and that one must be realistic and guide him down paths of lesser resistance so that a simpler and easier life will allow him to be happy. In short, Mother refused to allow anyone else to set my limits. Only I, and I alone, could find and define them. For that wisdom I am deeply grateful.

I owe Dad just as much, for he believed as strongly as Mother did in his deaf son's potential. Moreover, he was never a distant, remote figure, as were so many fathers of the time. Almost every spring and summer evening we'd play catch out front, even when I grew older and my fastball wilder, smokier, and more painful to catch. He'd coach third base for my Y club's softball games and volunteer as a timer at the endless swimming meets. He seemed to be everywhere.

He was always there even for my friends. In our early teens, my best friend, Sam Williamson, bit off more than he could chew when he bought a kit for a full-sized, fourteen-foot plywood Sailfish sailboat. His father, a brilliant professor who knew little of screwdrivers and saws (let alone formers and chines), was helpless. Dad came to the rescue and in a week's worth of evenings helped Sam get the boat together. And it was a job that looked as if it had been done by a professional.

One of Dad's most important legacies to me has been a deep appreciation for a job done right, with skill and exquisite, painstaking care. We spent many hours together in the basement building models and furniture and repairing bicycles and washing machines. Patiently he instructed me in the various uses of an awl and a spokeshave, a chisel and a backsaw, a plunger and a pipe wrench. The things we made always looked expertly done, not the clumsy products of a do-it-yourselfer.

He taught me, also, to make no little plans—especially when it came to home improvement. There was nothing we could not do so long as we had the proper tools, materials, and determination. Together we converted a back pantry into a powder room, brazing copper pipe and installing a heavy toilet. I was the one who scurried into the musty, cobwebby crawl space underneath the old pantry with the brazing torch; Dad, a six-footer, was just too big. I was so proud to be trusted with that important task that I momentarily lost my fear of spiders.

When we were very young, Buck and I were siblings of hackneyed normalcy. Like

85

brothers everywhere, we battled mightily. I still remember a particularly painful whaling Mother gave me when I was about four and he eight, after I resentfully laid a Louisville Slugger across his shins with all my strength. I have no recollection what the dispute was about, nor does he.

But as we grew older, Buck took a close interest in his little brother's welfare. For three years he was the counselor of my Y club. Like Mother and Dad, he believed in testing my capabilities, discarding those activities that seemed fruitless and encouraging those that seemed promising. He was a swimmer, too, and a counselor at Camp Echo. More than most little brothers, I followed in his footsteps. They were large ones, full of a loving encouragement that is rare among siblings.

My sister Debbie, thirteen years my junior, had yet to come along, and when she did, she would always be too young to have the sort of impact on my life that Buck had. Nonetheless, even as a very small child she made a difference—in an endearing sort of way. But I am getting ahead of my story.

As I entered junior high, there were two areas of endeavor in which I was superior to

86

most of my compatriots: reading and swimming. I felt strong and confident of my place in the scheme of things. Mother and Dad expected to have to battle the school authorities so that I could attend Haven Junior High with my friends near our house instead of Nichols Junior High with the other deaf children miles away on the south side of Evanston. But the officials assented, for my language development had progressed to a point where I could no longer be scored on standardized junior high reading tests. What had they to lose? Besides, Haven had an excellent speech teacher—not a teacher of the deaf, but what was then called a "speech correctionist."

Then I entered adolescence, that inescapable and implacable condition that tests the confidence of every youngster on earth.

—————5—————

Conventional wisdom holds that deaf youngsters' knowledge of sex lags far behind that of their hearing peers, simply because their shortcomings of language prevent them from acquiring information easily. Nonetheless, I entered eighth grade as learned, and as ignorant, about sex as any other thirteen-year-old of my acquaintance. When I was eleven Mother and Dad had given me a facts-of-life book for prepubescents, something that seemed to me better suited to a six-year-old with its irrelevant talk of pollen and eggs and its childish pictures of tadpoles and mice.

Like all my friends, I had obtained more scholarly instruction in the classroom of the gutter. A slightly older boy had informed me, in conspiratorial whispers, of the basic mechanics of the sexual act, and one my own age had introduced me to the pleasures of what then was called self-abuse. Moreover, I had discovered my parents' marriage manual in their bottom drawer.

Ideal Marriage was a classic of ornamental Victorian obfuscation by a Dr. T. H. Van de Velde, who never used one Anglo-Saxon word where three Latinate equivalents would do. I was fascinated by him, and appalled. He used such highfalutin terms as "intromission" and "coitus" and "phallus," forcing me, with almost every paragraph, to run downstairs to the living room to consult the big dictionary. His actual descriptions of "intercourse," a word he seems to have tried hard to avoid, taught me for the first time about irony, although it would be years before I came across the literary term.

And until I happened on the *Kama Sutra* late in high school, I thought, thanks to Van de Velde, that there were only two basic positions for the sex act, and that they had to be arranged with the help of a yardstick and a carpenter's level. Worse, every time Van de Velde got down to business, which wasn't often, he would stop to quote long and flowery passages from the classical literature of love, passages that were spiritual rather than carnal and seemed to have absolutely nothing to do with the matter at hand. He was the only writer I have ever encountered, other than Henry Miller, who could make sex sound like an energetic waste of time. I could not believe this book had helped my parents produce me, my brother, and my sister.

Of course I never made the connection between what I had read and had been told about and the demure young ladies at the ballroom dance classes we all attended every other Friday night in sixth and seventh grades. The white gloves and neckties, curtsies and bows of Miss Pocock's Fortnightly had to do with manners, not morals, and I would have been astonished if anyone had suggested any other relationship. I was having a wonderful time learning to dance, anyway, and I was good at it.

I won't say that the deaf as a group have rhythm, any more than do black people, but most of us can follow a beat as well as the hearing. We can often feel the music through the dance floor, and we also can pick up the tempo from watching others. At the waltz and fox-trot I was nimble on my feet, even graceful, much to the surprise of the parents who chaperoned the Fortnightlies, but my friends—both male and female—seemed to think it an unremarkable accomplishment. *They* were every bit as expert.

I also did my share of snuggling in Saturday afternoon movie-theater balconies, switching partners during intermissions, and played post office and spin the bottle during the boy-and-girl parties we hosted in our basements while our parents uneasily paced the kitchen floor above. It was at one of these parties that the light of lust finally shone upon me, during a long, slow, delicious bunny hug with a girl whose natural endowments surpassed those of her contemporaries.

But along with the rivers of hormones that began to course through my body came trickles of self-doubt, the curse of every adolescent. Some youngsters in the first stages of the condition agonize about their zits, buck teeth, knobby knees, big feet, curly hair, concave chests, and other perfectly normal physical shortcomings, magnifying them in their minds to nightmarish proportions. My particular grotesqueries were my lips and my speech.

I have what romance novelists sometimes call a "generous mouth," one whose adult dimensions a woman once described as sensual and desirable. The more I looked at my thirteen-year-old lips in the mirror, however, the more they resembled two slabs of liver hung out to dry. How, I began to wonder in my worst moments of dateless Friday night self-pity, could any girl want to be seen with *that?*

Furthermore, in junior high I had become more conscious of my speech. The youngsters I had known since the third grade were quite used to it, but most of my junior high classmates, drawn from all over the northern half of Evanston, were new to me, and there were a great many of them. For the first time I became aware of snickering whenever I spoke in class. It had happened before, but was so infrequent that I could dismiss the gigglers as ignorant louts. This time it seemed, in the self-magnification of the vulnerable young teens, to be happening every day. *And the girls were laughing, too!*

In the normal course of teenage events I would have fallen on my sword, writhed in agony for a while, then picked myself up and outgrown all the self-dramatization. But I was unlucky enough for my fears (hitherto confided to the bathroom mirror in absolute privacy) to be confirmed by an outside agency when I was at my most vulnerable.

One afternoon, sitting in my room, a fellow swimmer—one who, incidentally, suffered from a bad case of eczema—and I were talking about the prettier girls in our eighth-grade homeroom. I allowed as how I wouldn't mind going to a movie with Sally, who filled her blouse out to here and reportedly subscribed to a moral code down to there. "She won't go out with you," Bobby said firmly, doubtless echoing his own fears about *his* peculiarities. "You have big lips and you talk funny." The stake was driven hard and deep.

But I don't mean to leave the impression that I had been reduced to a sullen, withdrawn jelly of self-pity. Far from it. Between histrionic pangs there were races to be swum, games to be played, subjects to be studied —and lots of friends to do those things with. Concerned with their own adolescent worries, my chums didn't notice mine. At that age, a sudden and occasional shyness is hardly remarkable.

Besides, it wasn't all that apparent, even to me. But at school the more astute teachers soon did become aware that something was amiss. When called upon in class, I'd simply shrug and say, "I dunno—I really do." I wasn't going to give some smart-ass classmate from the other side of the city the smallest chance to laugh at my speech. I would, however, give plenty of attention to other students' answers, turning to the teacher and nodding sagely if they were correct. Expressing an intense interest in the subject at hand was enough to deceive everybody for a while, but as every bomber pilot knows, it's foolish to maintain strict radio silence in a swarm of Messerschmitts.

Nevertheless, I tried. On days when I had to deliver an oral report in class, I'd stay home sick. When assigned with another pupil to prepare a report, I'd do all the research and write the paper if the other kid agreed to stand up before the class and deliver it. It was the coward's way out. Had I had the courage, I knew, I could have stood up, spoken out, and stared down the dirty rotten no-goods who dared to snicker. My speech was not unintelligible. If one listened, it was as understandable as good English delivered with a heavy Eastern European accent. There really was nothing to be ashamed of—but how can that obvious truth be conveyed to a youngster who has convinced himself otherwise?

A few teachers took me aside and asked why I wouldn't speak in class, and I told them. They were not trained in the special psychology of the deaf, and I think they were largely nonplussed. They didn't press the issue. Perhaps they thought I'd be like everyone else and outgrow my adolescent fears. Maybe in time I would have, had there not been something else to contend with.

Because I had not grown up among other deaf children, I had managed to avoid acquiring most of the obvious "deafisms" —telltale physical characteristics of the handicap. These include exaggerated facial and bodily expressions, which deaf children brought up together, even in an oral environment, quickly learn in order to help them communicate with others. These often can seem grotesque to hearing people.

Another characteristic that makes the hearing uncomfortable is a tendency of many of the deaf to stand close to them in order to see their lips better, thus invading their "personal space." Then there is a tendency to shuffle the feet, to walk with heavy, clunky steps, and to drop objects upon tables, not realizing how much noise that makes. And a propensity for emitting what my family once called "funny noises."

Under stress or in moments of intense concentration, totally deaf people often unconsciously place their vocal cords and diaphragms under muscular tension while breathing. The result is a high, sometimes very loud nasal keening. We are unaware that we are making these noises, because the vibrations are too high-pitched for us to feel them in our throats. As a child I might occasionally issue a brief "funny noise," but a sharp glance from my parents or a muttered "Shut up!" from a friend in school would quickly stifle the little noon whistle. Maybe when that happened in class, someone would suppress a giggle, but I never noticed it. Such episodes seemed infrequent and trivial.

Until junior high. All too often I'd feel a punch in the shoulder from the kid across the aisle, look up from my book, and see everyone—*everyone!*—rocking over their desks in laughter, as if an unsynchronized wave of merriment had burst through the windows into the classroom. Up front, at her desk, the teacher would stare at me in puzzled horror. I'd bury myself in my book with sweaty, red-faced consternation. No hole was too deep to hide in. It would be many years before I trained myself out of this perfectly understandable but maddeningly embarrassing habit.

In the meantime, the damage was done. The once utterly open and friendly youngster was still in most ways outgoing, but when cornered by an obligation to speak in public turned shy and wary. Moreover, during my last year at Haven and my first at Evanston Township High School, a new problem surfaced. I was beginning to encounter practical limitations to the art of being a deaf person in the hearing world.

At fourteen, I was suddenly thrust into an unfamiliar situation for which my lipreading experience had not prepared me. Classes were much more formal, almost like lectures. We were now students, not pupils. We spent much less time working silently by ourselves at our desks. More often we would focus our entire attention on our teachers at their desks in the front of the room, droning on with the day's lesson, sometimes for an entire hour.

Hearing students can relax and listen passively, eyes focused in the distance, soaking up auditory information as it washes over them. Lipreaders, however, must concentrate on a small visual point—the teacher's lips—actively hunting for clues to what is being said. "Listening" of this kind is extremely hard work. We cannot look out the window briefly to rest our eyes or to digest a piece of information; if we do so, we might miss something important and even lose the thread of the discussion. If the teacher suddenly goes off on a tangent, we may flounder helplessly, searching for familiar words to help us get on track. The teacher might stop talking as someone in the rear of the room asks a question. Often I'd turn around, searching for the speaker, who might already have finished and lowered his arm. Quickly I'd whip back to the teacher, but the question would be answered, the subject perhaps changed anew.

But I was not entirely helpless. Early on I learned that many high school teachers of that age parroted the standard textbooks nearly word for word. In the first week of my freshman year, I discovered that my biology honors teacher—the head of the science department—might have been an unimaginative marionette of a lecturer, but he followed the textbook nearly verbatim, a chapter a day. I'd open it, place my finger on the words, and follow closely as he chattered on, page after page. The textbook not only was a "trot" for his lecture but also helped me learn his wooden-lipped way of speaking so that I could follow him more easily during laboratory periods, when the text wasn't of much help.

As the semester wore on, I found it more

relaxing to learn the biology text the night before class, then follow the teacher without the book the next day. But that was like listening to the playback of a recording, and before long became boring. Soon, confident that I knew the daily material well enough to be wholly prepared if the teacher sprang a surprise quiz upon us, I started reading popular novels in class, pretending I was following the teacher in the textbook. From time to time I'd glance up as if I were paying attention, then return to *Battle Cry.*

Mr. Jones may have been a drudge, but he was no fool. It was not long before he noticed that the little freshman among his mostly sophomore class was engrossed in something having nothing to do with biology. He did not, however, confront me directly. I don't think he quite knew how to deal with the situation; the few deaf students at Evanston High School in those days did not ordinarily take the same classes as their hearing compatriots. He took his case to Mr. Parsons, my homeroom teacher, who called me on the carpet one morning before classes.

"Mr. Jones says you're reading novels in his class," said Mr. Parsons, a brisk, businesslike man who believed in getting right to the point. For that reason—and because he was something of a showman, with a mobile face that was extremely easy to lipread —I had liked him from the beginning. "Yes," I said, "but Mr. Jones is kind of hard to understand. Besides, I'm getting a B plus in his class." I had been acing the quizzes and exams and doing somewhat less well in the lab work.

"Okay," said Mr. Parsons, to my utter surprise. He ushered me to the door of his office and in smiling dismissal shook my hand, always a sign of satisfaction with his students. I don't know what went through his mind that morning, but I sometimes think my high school teachers got together one day and decided to let the deaf freshman's academic performance determine how they were going to handle his eccentricities. So long as it was not perceived to be disrespectful, they would overlook my seeming inattentiveness. They were letting me find my own way, and for that I will always be grateful.

This is not to say that the teachers lacked any idea how to treat a deaf student. Most tried to broaden my opportunities for learning, helping me find other strategies to fill in the holes of my understanding. Sometimes I asked the teachers for extra reading because

I didn't understand the flow of conversation in class, and they willingly, even eagerly, found it for me.

They also seated me in the front row of the classroom, sometimes in the middle row closest to them, so I would have the best view of their lips. In some classes I'd ask for, and get, the first seat in the row closest to the window, so that the glare of daylight would be behind me, not in my eyes, when I turned to watch another student who was talking.

While most held me to the same academic standards as they did other students, my French teachers had to be pragmatic. While American English is spoken largely with the lips, French relies heavily on nasal sounds. While native French lipreaders, steeped in the culture, probably have no extraordinary difficulty, it is almost impossible for the untrained American lipreader to discern the nasal French "n" or the "r" rolled in the back of the throat. Moreover, I had enough trouble producing crisp and clear English speech; to expect me to speak French with any élan was obviously impractical. Hence the teachers graded me wholly on my reading and writing of the language and looked the other way when I spoke or attempted to lip-read it.

Only in mathematics did I have real difficulty. I have never been either adept at or interested in the subject, and so was disinclined to spend many hours filling in the gaps by poring over the textbook—which, anyway, was no model of clarity. In those days, too, there were no additional resources for slower learners. I had to depend on my understanding of my algebra and physics teacher, a decent instructor and a nice fellow who unfortunately fell into that 10 percent of Americans impossible to lipread. Algebra requires highly abstract thought, a careful building of concepts upon one another. Failing to understand one component meant failure to understand the whole.

From the hindsight of decades I can see that I should have asked for another instructor, one easier to lipread. I don't know why I didn't. Perhaps I thought I couldn't because the school policy was not to allow students to switch instructors, and I assumed that deaf students were included in that policy. So algebra and physics turned out to be a struggle; I managed to earn C's only with a lot of hard work and help from Dad, who in his day had been a whiz in math.

I did better, however, in geometry, partly because its abstractions are easily shown visually and partly because the teacher was a gifted Barnum who made every class a three-ring circus. Mr. Cady, a retired naval officer who had turned to teaching, was a tall, burly man who could, in an instant, switch from relaxed geniality to a stern air of command. In his class nobody dared to be a smartass. When he was annoyed he would bellow like a boatswain and when he was angry he would transfix the offender with a steady, baleful gaze from under hooded eyelids. It was like being fried by laser beams. But we liked him immensely, for he clearly loved us all, even the dumbest.

I sat in the front row and had an assigned spot on the blackboard close to his desk. Early in each class, as we worked our proofs in chalk, he had only to reach out a long arm to tap me on the shoulder and correct my errant computation. But as the period warmed up he'd get up from his desk and stride around the perimeter of the room, barking commands as if it were the bridge of a destroyer and he was setting drifting helmsmen back on course.

Across the room he'd spot me in an error. "Kisor! Kisor!" he'd shout at my back. Before an adjoining student could touch my wrist to warn me that the teacher wanted to speak to me, Mr. Cady would impatiently fire a blackboard eraser across the room to get my attention. He'd aim at a spot on the board two feet from my hand, but sometimes caught me on the back of the head instead. The whole class would crack up. So would he. And so would I. We were all laughing at him, not at me. I loved him for it.

I was not, however, blazing a trail through virgin forest. Another oral deaf student, three years older than I, had done brilliantly at Evanston High, ranking high in her class. (She went on to earn a doctorate and is now a practicing psychologist.) We did not know each other.

In the teenage pecking order of the times, seniors and freshmen rarely spoke to one another. And I think she may have been, like me, a deaf youngster who had never been acculturized to the community of the deaf, but had lived her entire life in the world of the hearing because there was no opportunity to encounter other deaf children of her abilities. Right or wrong, to us deafness probably would not have seemed much of a commonality. We were too busy finding our way in the hearing world.

I don't know whether she employed the same strategies I did, but her academic success may have led the school administration to assume that other deaf students could follow in her footsteps without special help, so long as they measured up to the standards set for hearing children. Certainly with me they seemed to maintain a hands-off, "don't fix it if it ain't broke" policy.

And so did Mr. Epler, my adviser, the specialist in deaf education. He was a quiet, comfortable, unflappable man who never condescended to his deaf students as if he believed them less capable than hearing ones. Many special education teachers believe the progress of their charges must conform to textbook precepts based on laboratory-revealed truth. Mr. Epler clearly didn't.

A good deal of his work lay in helping less accomplished deaf students with their academic courses, sometimes much of the day. But the only time I spent with him, other than occasional study-hall hours, was a weekly session in speech therapy, and when I entered my junior year, that ended. At the time I thought my communications skills were simply too advanced for him to improve and for that reason he assented to my taking conventional speech therapy with hearing students who lisped or spoke with foreign accents. That may have been true, but today I think there was more to it. His relaxed approach to me during those last two years of high school, I am convinced, was a studied one deliberately aimed at boosting my sometimes shaky self-reliance.

He would offer advice and counsel only when asked, and only if he thought it was necessary. When I confronted him with a problem, most often he would suggest that I try to solve it myself. For instance, I might not have understood all of a teacher's instructions on an assignment. To save a little time (and a potentially uncomfortable confrontation—in my misdirected pride I loathed the idea that my teachers might know I could not lipread every last word they said), I might ask Mr. Epler to call the teacher and get the details. He would gently suggest that if determining such academic details was a hearing student's responsibility, why couldn't it be mine as well? He seemed to believe, like Mother, that in the end only I could discover my limits, and in his subtle way he encouraged me to expand them as much as I could. I owe him a great deal.

In no manner was I a brilliant student. Throughout my high school career I earned respectable grades, mostly B's but with the occasional A and a few C's, chiefly in algebra and physics. This was in the laid-back 1950s, remember, when a decent C plus high school average could get you into a respectable college provided your Scholastic Aptitude Test scores were satisfactory. I was no slacker, but neither was I a humorless grind. There was just too much else to do. I was still active at the Y, and competitive swimming was a serious sport at Evanston High.

During my freshman year I was a starting freestyle sprinter and relay swimmer of decent speed, not a star but a dependable point earner. To my astonishment—and that of my teammates—I managed to win the eight-school Suburban League freshman 50-yard freestyle championship of 1954, in one of the slowest winning times ever recorded for that event. As a sophomore, I swam the third leg on the four-man varsity freestyle relay that finished third in the Illinois state meet, enabling Evanston High to win the team championship by a single point. That was the apex of my swimming career.

I had been a fast-developing physical specimen at thirteen and fourteen, but by fifteen my growth had topped out at a bit more than five feet six inches, and as we turned sixteen my taller and rangier teammates were taking the medals while I rode the bench as a secondstringer. They deserved to win; they trained a good deal harder than I did. Though swimming had been good to me, I had neither ambitions for stardom nor the physical equipment required for it. For years the sport had allowed me to compete with hearing athletes as an equal. Now it was time for me to do something else.

And that something was journalism. In freshman and sophomore English I showed a talent for writing, thanks to all that reading I had done as a child, and perhaps to heredity as well. My father, who was a businessman, not a trained professional writer, nevertheless had a talent for writing clear and lively prose, and if such a thing can be handed down through the genes, he passed it on to me. My sophomore English teacher, who apparently had never heard that the verbal skills of deaf students are supposed to be deficient, suggested to the journalism teacher that I might make a good candidate for her course as a junior. Though I had no idea what journalism entailed—the notion brought to mind a vague mental picture of a grizzled newspaperman in a fedora, dribbling cigarette ashes on his typewriter while barking commands into a telephone—I accepted her invitation to take the course. It was the best decision I had made in my young life.

Journalism, I learned quickly, did not involve merely the gathering of news by talking to people in person and on the telephone. For a deaf reporter the former was possible, though not very easy, but the latter was clearly impossible. Journalism, however, also involved a good deal of desk work. As a rewrite editor I found I had a definite knack for the shape of a story, for reducing it to its "who-what-where-when-why-how" components and reassembling these facts in the most efficient and pleasing manner. Once the stories were done, the next task was to assemble them, together with photographs, on the page, and then write a headline for each. For these things I also had a flair, and I also got along well with my fellow editors-in-training. At the end of the year I was appointed managing editor, or second-in-command, of the school paper.

As I grew older, sooner or later I would learn that conventional lay attitudes about deafness could severely—and unfairly—limit my horizons. The first occasion arose when at the end of my junior year I sought a summer job as a swimming pool lifeguard, and the experience was shattering.

Traditionally, Evanston High swimmers worked as lifeguards at country clubs so that they could train in the pools during their off hours. At the Y, I had earned all the qualifications: the Red Cross lifesaving and water safety instructor certificates. As a junior leader and swimming teacher I'd spent many hours sharing lifeguarding tasks around the Y pool. No one had ever suggested that deafness might be a hindrance to such a responsibility.

That spring, after the competition season, I asked Mr. Sugden, the Evanston High diving coach, for a guard's job the following summer at Sunset Ridge Country Club, where he ran the pool when school was out. "Sure thing," he said. "I'll set it up and get back to you." April arrived, then May, but I still did not hear from him. As June came closer I began to wonder why, and decided to seek out Mr. Sugden in his office to see if anything was wrong. Before I could do so, my parents, while attending a conference at the school, ran into the coach outside his office. "Henry's looking forward to his job with you this summer," Dad said.

Mr. Sugden looked at the floor in embarrassment. "I've wanted to tell him this," he said slowly, "but I can't figure out how to do it. You see, the club's board of directors won't let me hire him. They don't want a deaf lifeguard. They're worried about the lives of their children."

When my parents broke the news to me that evening, I was devastated. Nothing in my young life had prepared me for the rejections that were bound to come—especially arbitrary ones made in boardrooms by people I had never met, people who had never seen my capabilities, people who knew nothing about the deaf.

The notion of a deaf lifeguard is not as farfetched as it might seem. Bathers in trouble rarely, if ever, cry for help. They can't. They're choking on water and can't get out a sound. They either thrash madly or disappear quietly under the surface. That's why lifeguards are trained to scan the surface with their eyes. They're not listening for cries of "Help!" but watching for abnormal behavior in the water. When actual rescues aren't being conducted, lifeguarding is almost entirely a visual task.

111

As a group, I would later learn, the deaf are measurably superior to the hearing in the discernment of visual cues and the speed of responses to them. There's nothing super-human about this phenomenon. The loss of a sense forces the remaining ones to compensate, to stretch and exercise their capabilities beyond conventional thresholds. The average deaf person has the peripheral vision of a fish-eye lens, almost 180 degrees, and spots the tiniest movement within this range long before the average hearing person can do so.

In practical terms this superior visual acuity has led some automobile insurance companies in recent years to give sizable rate discounts to deaf drivers. Because the deaf are more visually alert behind the wheel than the hearing, we tend on the average to have fewer accidents, and thus are better insurance risks.

Many years later I laid this argument before an old childhood friend who had spent summers in college and afterward as chief of lifeguards at a string of beaches on Lake Michigan. He had known my capabilities at age sixteen, and he agreed with me, though he was careful to point out that a lifeguard's deafness could be a liability on a large lake-

front beach during a complex rescue operation involving several lifeguards and a series
of barked commands. That would, however,
be irrelevant at a small swimming pool
watched over by one or two lifeguards.

Of course, none of these arguments were
available to me at the time, and even if they
had been, nobody in a remote country-club
boardroom was going to listen to the wild
imaginings of a sixteen-year-old boy. Fortunately the staff at the Evanston Y had a
different viewpoint, and the hurt soon
healed.

For several years the staff at the Y had
watched me grow. I'd spent all my summers
at Camp Echo, first as a camper and then as
a "counselor-in-training" and as a member
of the kitchen crew. It was not difficult to
perform those responsibilities, and as Sam
Williamson and my other classmates applied
for jobs as full counselors, so did I. It never
occurred to me that my deafness might prove
a problem.

I don't know precisely how the Y officials
felt about my lack of hearing, but like the
school authorities, they seemed open-
minded enough to allow me to try one step
at a time, and if I negotiated it successfully,
to go on to the next. For four summers,

beginning in 1957, I played barracks ser-
geant to a dozen thirteen-and fourteen-year-
old hearing boys. I was, I think, as adept as
any other counselor, and the problems I had
seemed no different from anyone else's.

The only limitation the camp director im-
posed on me as a staff member was to excuse
me from lifeguarding duties. "I know you
can do the job," he said, "but if our insurance agent visited camp and found a deaf
guy being a lifeguard, what's he going to
think? He doesn't know you. He doesn't
have time to be convinced. He's going to
raise our rates through the roof."

It was easier for me to accept that pragmatic decision because I had another water-
front responsibility that was just as heavy:
while other counselors stood lifeguard duty
at the swimming area, I ran the water-skiing
program outside it. Much of the time I'd
drive the tow boat, instructing skiers with
hand signals. Sometimes I'd stand in the
water by the dock, helping novices learn the
complex and unfamiliar skill of getting up
on skis. Either way, I was responsible for
their safety. Nobody thought my deafness a
liability on the lake outside the boundaries
of the swimming area. Maybe the noise of
the tow boat's outboard motor made hearing

an academic issue. In any case, I never felt that anyone patronized my abilities.

Except for me. My long-simmering fear of speaking in public led me, that first summer as a counselor, to hobble myself needlessly. It happened when another counselor, a quiet and popular fellow of college age who suffered from a terrible stammer, froze one morning while trying to deliver the brief chapel homily with which the camp began its day. Nakedly, agonizingly, he stood before some 150 campers and counselors, the sweat bursting from his brow, trying to get out the first word. Minutes passed. He tried, and tried again, his face flushing with humiliation. Finally an older counselor stood up, squeezed his arm in commiseration, spoke a few words, and quietly dismissed the assembly.

A few of the younger campers may have snickered, but most of us sat in silent sympathy. We liked Pat, and we didn't know what to do. I suffered with him. I knew what was going through his mind. When he disappeared that night, abandoning his job to wrestle with his devils, I wasn't surprised. That could have been me up there, I thought. Maybe I would have frozen, too. The next day I stopped the director and told him that what had happened to Pat might happen to me, too. Could he excuse me from giving chapel and speaking before assemblies?

He did. That may not have been the wise thing to do. Maybe he should have insisted, "No, Hank. You can do it, and I don't want to hear any more of that nonsense." Just the same, there was nobody to blame but myself. I was responsible for my own actions.

Later in the summer, however, the director made an astute decision on the only other occasion at Camp Echo I can remember in which my deafness became an issue. The parents of one of my campers had heard that the young man charged with their son's care was deaf. They demanded that their boy be moved to another cabin under a more capable counselor, one who could hear. The director quietly reassigned the child without telling me why. Cabin reassignments weren't uncommon, but not for years did I learn the reason for that one. The director knew that a youth who was just turning seventeen was not mature enough to handle with equanimity that sort of ignorant thoughtlessness on the part of someone he had never met.

I was growing mature enough, however, for some new experiences. At siesta time one

August afternoon, an older counselor pressed a well-thumbed paperback into my reluctant hands. "Give it a try," he insisted.

The book was *The Grapes of Wrath* by John Steinbeck, of whom I had only vaguely heard. To me, an indifferent schoolboy, the cover did not look promising. Depression? Dust bowl? Tenant farmers? Okies? Old stuff long forgotten. Who cares?

Within an hour I was electrified. Almost all night I sat up with a flashlight in the darkened cabin, my charges sleeping quietly while I read of the trials of Steinbeck's Joad family. *The Grapes of Wrath* opened my young eyes to many things. For the first time I learned of my country's appalling history of labor exploitation and the blinkered refusal of its economic royalists to appreciate the misery of the dispossessed. The novel's graphic depiction of human dignity in the face of adversity showed me, a white-bread middle-class Midwestern suburbanite of the Eisenhower Age, that the poor and unlettered were capable of astonishing heroism, and that it could be celebrated in epic fashion.

For the rest of that summer I devoured as much Steinbeck as I could get my hands on. One by one I read his other fine novels of the 1930s—*Tortilla Flat, In Dubious Battle,* and *Of Mice and Men.* Steinbeck became my new hero, replacing Joe DiMaggio. For the first time the urgency of literature had struck me.

Expanding on this discovery, however, had to wait. When September rolled around and school resumed, I was suddenly and to my considerable surprise a prominent member of the senior class, one whispered about by goggle-eyed freshmen and envious sophomores as I passed them in the hall. But I was no longer the "deaf kid," as I had imagined my schoolmates had condescendingly classified me. I was the managing editor of the school paper, a true celebrity. Not necessarily because of any cogent wisdom or witty repartee in my columns, but because of one of the perks of the job. I was one of a handful of students who held a coveted "open pass" that allowed me to leave the campus at any time during my lunch and study periods, presumably on official school business, but sometimes just to enjoy a cigarette. In those days student smoking was strictly forbidden, with frequent detentions for those caught stealing a puff on school property. Most tobacco addicts had to suffer without a fix from eight in the morning to three in the afternoon. Often, however, pretending to be off checking proofs at the printer's or interviewing a prominent downtown merchant, I'd drive around the block furiously inhaling a Lucky Strike, then return in plenty of time for the next class. (Not for nineteen years would I succeed in kicking the habit.)

Naturally this new prominence did wonders for my maturing ego, and I was as comfortable as any fellow senior, airily treating underclassmen with benign contempt. Why, I even spoke up in class on occasion, though I still hated and dreaded delivering any sort of formal address, and was an expert at ducking that responsibility. I had also begun to outgrow my pimply awkwardness with girls and had started dating regularly, though not as earnestly as some other seniors. Like most of the men in my family, I was a late bloomer in my relations with the opposite sex. Not until well into my college career would I enjoy my first grand passion. Nonetheless, I moved easily among a variety of social circles, although I lacked the smooth, polished manner of the truly self-assured. I even had a splendid time at the senior prom—a highly charged event that often tested the social and emotional mettle of youths in the 1950s.

On graduation day I ranked a respectable 90th in a class of 591 students. The nightmares of eighth grade seemed far in the distance.

Like every college freshman of any era, I had an enormous adjustment to make when I arrived at Trinity College. No longer was I a member of the elite, a standout in the crowd. As high school seniors, the three hundred members of the new Class of 1962 at this distinguished "little Ivy" men's college in Hartford, Connecticut, had been proud cocks of the walk. Now we all were hatchlings again, scratching nervously for our places in a strange new barnyard.

Half were public high school graduates, the other half products of Eastern prep schools. Many of us "publics" harbored vague feelings of social and intellectual inferiority toward the wealthy men's sons who wore the old school ties of Choate, Exeter, and Andover. How could we possibly compete with these blond young Apollos who drove Jaguars, quoted Cicero, dated Muffys from Smith and Graemes from Holyoke, and looked forward to instant vice presidencies in the family firms? So overwhelming a challenge did that seem that it never occurred to me to worry about making the grade as a deaf student at a hearing college.

I had chosen Trinity for three reasons: because it was small and intimate, with an excellent student-professor ratio; because it had awarded me a partial scholarship, which I badly needed; and because Buck had made a bold mark there. The previous June he had graduated in a gust of glory, with honors in economics and a Phi Beta Kappa key. Moreover, he was a member of Medusa, the elite palace guard of nine seniors—the highest honor a Trinity undergraduate could achieve. He had also won a Woodrow Wilson fellowship for postgraduate study at Northwestern.

But I was not fretting about living up to that example. Luckily I had never suffered from the second-son complex. Certainly I'd followed in Buck's large footsteps down many trails, but instead of resenting the inevitable comparisons other people made between us, I welcomed them. I felt that his success had established a family tradition, that people would measure my performance not as a deaf student but as a Kisor, and that their expectations therefore would be high.

I was proud to be Buck's little brother and grateful for his achievements.

In the beginning, though, Mike Mather wasn't so proud to be my roommate. Just before he arrived on campus from his home in Perrysburg, Ohio, the dean's office had asked him to drop by before going to his new room in Elton Hall. "You're going to be rooming with a deaf student," the dean told Mike. "We felt it only fair to tell you before you meet him." Mike was thunderstruck. He had all the usual worries of a brand-new freshman, but he had never dreamed that he would have to play nursemaid to a . . . *cripple!*

When he walked into our room, his expression was a woebegone mixture of horror and resignation. "Hello, Mike," I said cheerily, bubbling over with nervous enthusiasm. "Glad to meetcha. Had lunch yet? Want to grab a burger?"

"Uh . . . yeah," he said. "No. Yeah. Huh?" The cripple *walked!* The cripple *talked!*

Weeks later we would both laugh as Mike told the story of our meeting to a knot of fellow freshmen in a tavern on the edge of campus. We never became fast friends, for he was more mature than I, deeply serious about his studies, and always concerned about money. I, in turn, believed in taking time out to play and never worried where my next dime would come from, even though I was also a scholarship student. Somebody or something, I reasoned, would provide.

Yet Mike and I shared a mutual respect; after our first week together, he later told me, he never again felt that a special responsibility had been dumped upon him. We remained roommates our sophomore year, in a prized four-man suite on the historic old quadrangle, but a few days after Christmas break that year, we received a solemn letter from Mike telling us he had simply run out of money and had had to withdraw to attend a less expensive public college near his hometown.

Though the dean never thought I'd need a nursemaid, he didn't necessarily share all the high expectations I had for myself. He knew certain adjustments would have to be made, though he probably did not know exactly what they would be. Trinity had not had a deaf student since the middle of the nineteenth century, but, like the officials at Evanston High, the dean seemed to believe in taking things a step at a time, letting problems arise and then dealing with them as appropriate. I was a *tabula rasa,* but Trinity let me hold the chalk. It was all up to me— with a little discreet help.

The first problem arose during the first week of classes. *"Comment vous appelez-vous?"* asked the professor of French. "What?" I replied, dumbfounded. I still could not lipread *un mot* of the language, let alone speak it with any facility. This was not going to work, the professor knew. He taught his course entirely in French, and expected his students to respond in it. Not that I wanted to take the course; a year of a foreign language was one of the requirements for graduation.

After a hurried meeting with the dean, the head of the language department called me in. "We've decided to design a whole new course for you," he said grandly. It was a reading course, and with his guidance I would choose literary works to study, then write weekly reports—in French, of course.

At first I was unhappy. Already, I thought, I was falling short of expectations. I wanted to measure up, to be judged by the same standards as other freshmen. As time went on, however, and I dove deep into Ca-mus's *L'Etranger,* then the comedies of Molière and the philosophy of Sartre, I grudgingly appreciated the professor's wisdom. Not being able to converse in French didn't mean I couldn't stretch my intellectual wings in the language as widely as others did. I grew to love the reading, challenging in its own right, and earned respectable marks on my reports, graded as rigorously as those of other freshmen. I could still hold my head high.

Calculus was something else. All freshmen had to pass a semester of it. I was horribly unprepared, for I had not had a mathematics course during my senior year in high school. At first I managed to stay abreast, earning passing grades, but as the year went on I floundered further and further behind.

Soon my exam average had fallen below 70. Trinity's grading was on the percentage system. Marks in the 90s were the equivalent of an A; those in the 80s, B; those in the 70s, C; and anything above 60 was a D but passing. I worked harder and harder, but my average crept lower and lower. I was in an honest-to-God jam. If I failed the course, I wouldn't be able to retake it, for I'd have lost my scholarship and could not afford to remain at Trinity.

Robert Stewart, who taught my section of

the course, had just earned his doctorate and was a brand-new instructor at Trinity. He was a good teacher, and I did not have great difficulty lipreading him, for he was easy to understand and made sure to face me whenever he discussed the equations he had written on the blackboard. When led step by step through the calculations, I could follow the rigorous mathematical logic. But my understanding was simply too weak for me to fly solo in examinations.

After a soft word from the dean, who had seen the midterm grades, Stewart called me aside after class one morning. "You need tutoring," he said. "I think if we work together a couple of times a week, we can get you through this course." But how could I afford to pay for the tutoring? It wasn't inexpensive, and as a scholarship student I had already stretched every dollar as far as it could go. "We'll worry about that later," Stewart replied.

I have yet to receive his bill, and I'll happily pay it if it ever comes—with compound interest. For I squeezed through the final examination with a 64, kept my scholarship, and remained at Trinity. (Stewart is now head of the Trinity mathematics department.)

Things went well, however, in my remaining courses—surveys of English literature and European history. Though they were called "lecture courses," the bulk of the work was in reading and in term papers. These required no additional effort beyond the assignments, and from the beginning I was able to earn marks in the low and middle 80s, quite respectable for a freshman. In these courses I learned a new strategy: finding the student who took the most copious lecture notes and asking if I could sit next to him and copy them as he took them down. Nobody ever demurred.

Today deaf students at hearing colleges often use "note packs" of carbon sheets sandwiched with paper, the whole to be slipped under the top sheet of a hearing student's notebooks. As the hearing student converts the professor's lecture into notes, a copy is automatically and effortlessly made for the deaf student, who may or may not be sitting next to the note taker—or even be present at the lecture. Had these been available to me, however, I doubt that I'd have used them. The act of writing notes helped me retain the material; as I took down the professor's facts and comments, I could digest them thoroughly. Besides, some professors were fairly easy to lipread, especially those in the history department. For some reason, many historians seem to pay attention not only to the art of writing history but also to lecturing about it, with dramatic flourishes. I reveled in their courses.

Many of my note-taking benefactors also made certain to commit the professors' jokes, awful though they might be, to paper so that I could enjoy—or suffer from—them as much as the rest of the class. And they never asked anything in return.

At some point in the lives of all college students—if they are lucky—a love of learning for its own sake knocks on the door of the mind. The long hours of studying no longer seem an onerous duty but are a joy that fills the day. That is the first stride toward a civilized mind, and toward the end of my second year at Trinity it came calling.

The exact moment I've long forgotten. But it probably occurred sometime during my reading of Thomas Wolfe's *Look Homeward, Angel,* an autobiographical novel that justly has been disparaged as a bombastic melodrama of the throes of post-adolescence, suitable only for sophomores. But I *was* a sophomore. The word may connote a know-it-all without a shred of experience, but also means someone on the verge of shedding foolishness for wisdom. Not since *The Grapes of Wrath* had jarred my sixteen-year-old, middle-class complacency had a book so affected me, and I devoured as much of Wolfe as I could. I barely noticed that *Of Time and the River* and *The Web and the Rock* were thinly disguised rewrites of Wolfe's first novel, their heroes plagued by the same callow self-obsession. Wolfe's characterizations may have been juvenile, but his prose style was hypnotic. I studied his rolling, sonorous sentences, marveling at the way they often started on tiptoe, almost hesitantly, then strode and sprawled as if exalted.

Like every undergraduate who first experiences literary intoxication with Wolfe, I tried to adopt his dramatic style. Fortunately, I was unsuccessful. I was still branded by the *Time-Life* journalese that had entered my sensibility at an early age, with backward-running sentences and stampedes of adjectives trampling lonely nouns. A brief infatuation with Hemingway's spare, skeletonized style followed, and that may have helped.

What did take root was a love for the way words sounded. I could not, of course, hear them—the auditory spectrum was beyond my competence. But words have definite and distinct vibrations and I could roll them across my tongue, feeling how they thrummed on my throat, cheeks, teeth, lips, and nose. Nose. Knows. The nose knows. The *nnozze knowzz*. My nostrils would resonate with each "n," my lips with each "o." The "z" brought forth a delicious low buzz on the tips of the front teeth.

All this I could "hear" on the tympanum of my mind. Was this just imagination, or a genuine echo from somewhere deep in the cells of memory, a soft electrical charge still strong enough to preserve some of the lost hearing of the precocious three-year-old who could belt out every verse of "The Eyes of Texas Are Upon You"? I began to say the words as I wrote them, softly sounding out each sentence as it appeared on the page.

In the beginning the result was cacophonous, for I was trying to pack a whole orchestral composition into a sentence. Not for a long time would I learn that one first had to master stress and tempo, meter and melody—the entire spectrum of English prosody—while at the same time striving for simplicity and clarity. That lay largely in the future. But the embarrassingly long, intricate, and exquisitely balanced sentences with which I began to dress my literature and history papers were at least a start.

By the end of the sophomore year every student's academic strengths and weaknesses ought to be evident, and mine were. Mathematics and science clearly were not my métier. Galvanized by literature, I chose English for a major, but with a strong minor in history. Those should be unsurprising choices. Except for drama, both are solitary disciplines. Excellence in them is measured by breadth and depth of research and in the resultant written examinations and papers.

Hearing and speaking are irrelevant. In those courses of study my deafness was neither hindrance nor asset, except possibly in the early habits I had acquired while still in high school—the habits of extra reading and writing to compensate for not being able to lipread my teachers consistently. Earlier than most other students, perhaps, I had learned how to start researching a question —how, in short, to use a library. To a student, deafness is not always a disadvantage.

Neither is it an advantage. It seems logical to think that the deaf can concentrate more intensely than the hearing—that we can shut out distractions more easily than others and get more work done in a given amount of time. That's not true at all. We're sensitive to many of the same noises that drive other people crazy. The booming bass of the super-stereo in the next room reverberates on the floor, tingling the soles of our feet, and we're just as conscious of that as you are of the assault on your ears. We can feel dump trucks rumbling by on the street underneath our dorm windows and the nervous knee drumming of the student on the other side of the library table.

But we can't identify many of those noises, and that's what's so maddening. Suppose a heavy thump, then a skittering dribble jolts you, a hearing scholar, out of a reverie as one rowdy student body-checks another into the wall, then both laughingly scramble after a loose football bouncing down the dormitory hall. "Shaddup!" you'll shout in irritation, instantly recognizing the racket for what it is, and then return to your work.

But I must get up from my desk and go find out what made all that tumult. Has someone returning from a fraternity party passed out and fallen on the floor? Is someone trying to get my attention by body-slamming my locked door? "What the hell's going on?" I demand as I whip open the door and behold the grinning pile of students on the floor before me. They look up at me in amazement. How could *he* . . . ?

What's more, they want to know, how am I so easily aware when someone walks quietly and unseen into the room behind me? I smile. Some secrets are worth keeping, some mysteries worth maintaining. I don't tell them that perhaps it's just the almost imperceptible puff of air ruffling the hair on the back of my neck as a caller opens the door. Or a familiar creak of a floorboard by the doorway. Or the slight reflection of a glint of light from my reading lamp on the moving doorknob in the glass of a framed photograph that hangs on the wall just above my desk. Sometimes I'm reading a newspaper and suddenly, on the sensitive membrane of an open page, feel the vibrations of a hearty basso "Hello!" from behind me.

I also don't tell them that all these stratagems can fail me. Sometimes, if I succeed in attaining an intense trance of concentration, I unconsciously shut off all my receptors, tactile and visual. You could play hockey with anvils two feet from my head and I would not twitch. When I am deep into such spells, someone who does not know I am deaf might approach my back unseen and speak to me. When I do not answer, he'll repeat his statement. If I ignore him a third time, he'll repeat it again, with mounting irritation. I always seem to awaken and turn around innocently at the precise moment the other fellow growls, "What's the matter? Are you deaf?"

Sadly and sweetly—for there is no other way, if the poor fellow is not to dissolve in a puddle of resentful embarrassment—I nod, smile, and say, "Yes."

I'm convinced that most students at Trinity regarded me benignly, with a mixture of respect for my academic performance, approval of my independence from my handicap, and amusement over my parlor tricks. I was by no means a Big Man on Campus, but neither was I a wallflower. Two fraternities—my brother's rambunctious Sigma Nu and the more sedate Theta Xi across the street—offered me pledge bids, and I accepted the latter. For two years the fraternity would be the center of my social life and the classroom for a new course of instruction—not an academic offering, but a practical survey in the stresses of interaction between the hearing majority and the deaf minority.

Human beings, as individuals, are inclined to be kindly, compassionate, and tolerant. Most hearing people, in my experience, can readily form friendships with a deaf person —provided that they have something in common and can communicate with one another. With such one-to-one relationships I have always been comfortable. So long as the other person faces me, perhaps speaking a bit more slowly than usual, and can give me undivided attention, we can connect. In the beginning there might be mild unease with each other's unfamiliar way of speaking, but with a little time and experience, we learn to talk with each other smoothly and easily, letting down our guard and accepting things as they are.

In groups, however, such swift lines of communication tend to break down. The hearing find others like them easy to talk with; communication with a deaf person requires conscious effort. So involved in their conversation do groups of hearing people become that they tend to forget that a deaf person might be with them, needing help. To the lipreader, people in group conversations talk rapidly, the conversational ball rocketing from mouth to mouth almost faster than the eye can see. It's hard for a lipreader to jump into such a conversation, and when one does not contribute to it, one simply is not present in the minds of others.

One night the Theta Xi brothers sent their pledge class of nine sophomores out on a scavenger hunt. Our quarry was chosen with typical fraternity-boy humor: a dead cat and other objects too tasteless to mention. We piled into a car and drove around Hartford searching for objects. Having scoured the city for all it could offer, we headed into the Connecticut countryside. I sat in the crowded back seat of the darkened car, understanding nothing of what the other pledges said. It was nearly pitch black.

As we drove aimlessly, the minutes rolling by, I began to grow impatient. "Would somebody turn on the light and tell me what's going on?" I said. Nobody answered. A few moments later I said, "Hey, what *are* we doing?" The fellow sitting next to me gave me a none too gentle elbow in the ribs.

Five minutes later, quite at the end of my patience and beginning to fret—two hours of seemingly purposeless wandering about the boondocks is bound to raise a twinge of worry—I said, "Goddamnit. Why won't anybody tell me what's going on?" The dome light flashed on. A pledge sitting in the center of the front seat turned and said angrily, "If you don't shut up, I'll punch you in the mouth." I sat back, stunned and hurt, and said nothing to anyone until we returned to the fraternity house in the small hours.

I never did find out what was going on in the car that night. Perhaps the pledges were tired and upset over their lack of success in tracking down the items on the scavenger list and had run out of patience and tolerance for anything, let alone a deaf fellow pledge. Perhaps I unwittingly said the wrong things at the worst possible moments. Whatever the truth, what was obvious was that the threads of communication I had spun with them as individuals were too fragile to survive in a group under stress. But we never did return with a dead cat. We were too kindhearted to kill one.

These were not cruel and thoughtless people, but intelligent young men who, beyond our brief intellectual conversations, had had no experience with the deaf. They simply assumed that I, as a fellow Trinity student and Theta Xi pledge, would share their capabilities. Only with experience could they learn my limitations—and I was still learning them myself.

Although the episode would stick in my memory, I couldn't stay dismayed for long. Besides, on ordinary (and well-lighted) occasions, I managed to get along well with my fraternity brothers. At the end of our junior year I campaigned for and was elected corresponding secretary—a largely ceremonial position that involved writing occasional letters to college and city officials and alumni. For nearly three years, my time at Trinity settled into a mostly normal, ordinary—and happy—life.

And for the first time in my young manhood, I fell in love, into the kind of all-consuming grand passion that falls just short of obsession. In high school and the first two years at Trinity I had continued to date, even to the point of "going steady" once or twice, but my relationships with the opposite sex had remained callow. Girls were either good buddies or objects of lust.

This was, after all, the Eisenhower Age, an era that still prized virginity. Young women armored themselves before dates, wearing heavy panty girdles below and cantilevered, hard-plastic constructions called

"Merry Widows" above. We young men boasted about our sexual activities in baseball clichés. "First base" was, of course, a kiss. "Second base" was those treasures guarded by the Merry Widows. "Home runs" were rare and much lied about. Like most, I had been a low-average spray hitter occasionally lucky enough to stretch a single into a double.

Rachel was the same age—twenty—and a student at Tufts University near Boston, three hours east of Hartford. We had met the summer between our sophomore and junior years at Camp Echo. I had been drawn instantly to this extraordinary girl from Lake Forest, a wealthy North Shore suburb. She was tall and pretty, with a warm, friendly manner, a dimpled smile that could disarm a gunman, and a Junoesque body. She was also one of the most dynamic people I had ever met. Not only could she hold her own in free-for-alls about Heidegger or Manet, but she was also a gifted dancer who often starred in musicals at Tufts, as well as a class officer and an accomplished student.

How Rachel was able to juggle all these things and carry on a heavy weekend relationship with a student at another college I'll never quite know. But we managed to see each other almost every weekend, thanks to buses between Hartford and Boston and the extraordinary generosity of a fraternity brother and roommate, Sam Curtis, who was not averse to loaning a good friend the keys to his brand-new Volkswagen.

That autumn was a classical college idyll, with fraternity parties, football weekends, and passionate nights in off-campus motels. It was one of the happiest times of my young life. The problems of deafness seemed irrelevant, a thing of the past. Rachel and I were, in the romantic conceit of the young, a single entity, each half of which could anticipate the every feeling and thought of the other.

First passions always end painfully, and mine was no different. At some point in our relationship, I think, Rachel began to realize that the mysterious, miraculous abilities of the deaf young man with whom she was smitten were in truth not all that extraordinary. He had genuine limitations. He did not have the social polish of the other young men she knew. With her friends and family he was shy, awkward, and uncommunicative. Nothing in his manner suggested that he might be bound for the boardroom, to become a captain of industry who could provide a comfortable life.

Rachel came from a well-to-do family, one that measured success by income and social position. I had neither of those, nor aspirations in those directions—or any other, for that matter. At twenty I was not mature enough to know what I wanted to do with the rest of my life. One day I might talk about attending law school, the next about studying archaeology, the next about going immediately to work as an insurance man. Or maybe I might become a poet. I was no model of stability.

Rachel's father, the founder and president of a successful manufacturing company, could not stand me, and I cannot blame him. I couldn't lipread him easily and, perhaps more unconsciously than consciously, avoided talking to him whenever I visited Rachel's house. Evasiveness is hardly a desirable attribute in the character of a prospective son-in-law—especially one who seemed never to have anything interesting to say, let alone a useful future. Besides, they were Jewish and I an unchurched Protestant—and in those days, religious differences were much more important to the parents of young people than they are today.

If Rachel's mother, however, harbored negative feelings about the young man who was so clearly crazy about her daughter, she kept them well hidden. She was kindly and considerate toward me, and we had many long talks while I waited for Rachel to come downstairs to go out on a date with me. I could see that Rachel had inherited not only her father's drive but also her mother's warm curiosity.

Matters came to a head at the end of the summer between our junior and senior years. Rachel and her family—including her two younger sisters—headed for Europe. For the first time in six years, I did not return to Camp Echo. I wanted to do something different, to enjoy new experiences. Sam Curtis and I decided to drive west, to earn money as fruit and vegetable pickers in the San Joaquin Valley of California. My parents were dismayed, but theirs was a quiet and unexpressed disapproval, because they knew that if I was to grow into an independent adult, I needed to make mistakes and learn from them.

As they expected, Sam and I didn't pick a single bean, but we enjoyed ourselves all the same. In his Volkswagen we drove southwest to Los Angeles down romantic Route

66. We camped by the edge of the Grand Canyon, where we learned for the first time the deeper implications of the word "immense." We fought off a homosexual motelkeeper in San Bernardino and went deep-sea fishing off Santa Catalina Island with my great-uncle, a childless, adventurous man who loved his many nephews as if they were his own sons.

We slept under the stars in a high-country campground in Yosemite National Park, where one morning I spoke crossly to Sam because he had failed to wake me when a black bear a few yards away batted a garbage can around as if it were a medicine ball. How could he have let me sleep through such an adventure? He was, he said, too frightened to move. We got drunk in Reno, roasted in Death Valley, and awoke shivering in snow-covered sleeping bags in a place in the Colorado Rockies called Neversummer Pass.

When our money ran out we returned to Evanston, where we replenished our exchequer running informal swimming classes for neighborhood children at the beach; ours was really a babysitting service, but we did teach some youngsters to swim. Once again flush, we drove to New Orleans and sipped espresso and ate *beignets* at the Morning Call, where we imagined ourselves poets. And as August neared an end and our stake dwindled, Sam dropped me off in Evanston, then returned to his Connecticut home for a few days before the academic year began. We were high as kites. We had seen the world and henceforth nothing would chain us to the old farmstead.

Then Rachel and her family came home from Europe. Much to the displeasure of her father, I was waiting at the door of their home as they arrived from O'Hare. Rachel took my hand as the others unloaded the taxi. "Let's go for a walk, Hank," she said, without inviting me inside. As we walked, she told me that she and her sisters had had long talks about me in Paris and Rome. They had wept, she said, as they compared my amiable charm with my prospects as a potential husband and breadwinner. "Hank, you are deaf," said Rachel, who had always been blunt and honest in our relationship. "You're a wonderful guy and I'll always love you. But how are you going to make a living? What are you going to be able to do? You yourself don't know. I need something more than that."

Naturally I tumbled into a maelstrom of affection, confusion, anger, and denial. I had loved Rachel for her frankness, and I still did, even if her words hurt mightily. Years later, putting myself in her place, I had to admit that what she said carried more than a germ of truth. Even at twenty-one I was too immature, too unformed to have any sort of prospects. Maybe I was bright and funny and a joy to be with, but I had no idea what I was going to do after graduation. And my by now habitual reticence with people I did not know was not an encouraging sign.

Rachel, bless her heart, had attempted to end the relationship as kindly as she could, but also as cleanly and surgically as possible, so there would be no mistake in her meaning. Our old relationship was over, she said, but we could still "be friends." Grudgingly and slowly I accepted the situation, and we did remain friends. From time to time during our senior year we met for a chat. One afternoon a few weeks before graduation, as we sat comfortably together in the foyer of her dormitory at Tufts, she confessed her worries for her future. "If only I could get married!" she said. "What about *me?*" I thought—but with only the briefest twinge of regret.

We remained in occasional friendly touch for a couple of years, until she married. She still lives in Lake Forest, a homemaker and wife of a wealthy man, mother of four, active in civic and social affairs. I have not seen her for more than a quarter of a century, but my memories of her are fond ones, and I dearly hope that she is happy. My only regret for her is that she was born ten years too soon. If she had grown up in America during the feminist revolution of the early 1970s, she might have directed that awesome energy down avenues that could have made her famous.

For two years I had given little thought to my deafness, to the idea that it could have consequences that would affect my life adversely. Now, thanks to being dumped by the woman I loved, it was back under my skin, gnawing away at my confidence. I became ever more conscious, ever more ashamed of my deaf speech. One night at a formal fraternity meeting, it was my task as corresponding secretary to read the lengthy text of a letter from a college official to the forty or so assembled brothers. It was the first time since I had been pledged two years earlier that I had to speak before a group. There was no honorable way to avoid the awful duty.

My mouth dried. My pulse hammered. My armpits dampened. My throat tensed. As I read, my voice turned thin and reedy. I panted as I continued, stopping to take a breath after almost every phrase. I must have been wholly unintelligible. I looked up. The brothers stared at me in amazement. I pressed on. They began to laugh—not so much in merriment, perhaps, but nervously, uncomprehendingly. I struggled through to the end, my face hot with shame, the seat of my trousers sticking sweatily to the chair.

Quietly, as I gazed down at the table, the fraternity's president continued the business of the meeting. A few moments later, when he paused, I raised my hand. "Point of personal privilege," I said, the *Robert's Rules of Order* euphemism for absenting oneself to answer a call of nature. I left the house and walked back to my dormitory.

Abandoning a formal fraternity meeting in such a manner was a severe breach of ritual, an offense for which the president was empowered to levy a cash fine or even a suspension. *"Point of personal privilege, Hank?"* he said with heavy sarcasm later that night, after he had tracked me down in my room. "Come *on!*" But he added, more gently, "Look, I know what's going through your mind. Come back to the house tomorrow and let's forget it."

I couldn't. Ten days later I wrote a formal letter to the president announcing that I was "going inactive," relinquishing my membership. I had persuaded myself that I was doing so because the whole notion of college fraternities was based on a shallow and immature camaraderie, that it was undemocratic and perpetuated the worst form of social exclusion. The real reason was that I had lost my nerve. I had given in to my seething frustration over my speech.

To make matters worse, that spring brought the corporate recruitment season for graduating seniors. I joined everyone else in the interviews, although I had no idea what I was qualified for. I did not know what questions to ask, how to comport myself. Always ill at ease, I sweated and stammered through dozens of interviews. I behaved like a nervous high schooler rather than a self-assured college senior about to graduate. And out of perhaps thirty interviews came one follow-up invitation to visit the home office. One out of thirty! My friends, meanwhile, were being wined and dined by nearly every company they talked to, some of them being offered positions in training programs on the spot.

The sole company to ask me back was the Penn Mutual Life Insurance Company. I flew down to Philadelphia, talked inconclusively with a few executives, and scored abominably on the mathematics aptitude test. In the end the personnel director said, "You don't really want to be an insurance man, do you?" He had thought they might make an actuary out of me. "No, I guess not," I said, feeling thoroughly sorry for myself as I gazed out the window at ships lining the quays of the port of Philadelphia. "I'm going to go to sea."

A week or so later the dean called me into his office. "I understand you're planning to go to sea, Henry," he began. I stood puzzled for a moment, then remembered, and blushed. Those guys at Penn Mutual had ratted on me! "No, Dean," I said, chuckling weakly, and explained it all. "I just said the first dumb thing that came to mind."

To the dean I was not the first Trinity senior to suffer a *crise de confiance* on the eve of graduation, when we at last fled—or were pushed from—the nest. "*You* may be worried, Henry," he said, "but *I* have confidence in you. You'll be all right. I think you'll soon hear some good news that'll surprise you. Now let me ask you: What else have you considered?"

There wasn't much. My English adviser had suggested library school, but I wasn't interested in a dry and musty career in lonely book stacks. The University of Edinburgh had accepted me for graduate study, but I hadn't the wherewithal to get to Scotland, let alone any idea what I might do with a graduate diploma in literature. And there was the Medill School of Journalism at Northwestern University, which had offered me an assistantship—one that I had turned down. I wasn't cut out for journalism, I thought.

Thankfully someone else held the opposite view. For years an old family friend, David Botter, had watched me grow up. A onetime senior editor at *Look* magazine and a professor of journalism at Medill, he had often thought that I might make a good newsman, thanks in part to my having been the managing editor of the Evanston High School paper. He did not believe that deafness was necessarily a hindrance in certain aspects of the profession.

Though journalism no longer held any interest for me, during Christmas vacation that senior year I spoke with him and, at my parents' urging, filled out an application for the graduate program. But when the letter of acceptance arrived in the spring, together with a note saying that I'd been awarded an assistantship that would pay most of the tuition, I wasn't interested. Almost all my friends at Trinity were going into banking or insurance, and I thought that was where I had to go, too. I wrote back to Medill declining with thanks.

I strongly suspect that Botter and the Trinity dean conspired to persuade Medill to hold open both the place in the graduate class and the assistantship until my good sense got the better of me. Almost on the day before graduation, it did. With nothing else in sight on the employment horizon, I wrote back to Botter asking if my application could be reinstated. Not only was the place still open, he replied, but why not begin with a couple of summer courses at Medill and see how I fared?

I was stunned at my good fortune. *Somebody* still believed in me.

But that was not the good news the dean had alluded to when he had summoned me to his office. The day before commencement, I learned that I was graduating with honors in English, thanks to a senior thesis I had written on Faulkner's Snopes trilogy the previous semester. ("Absolutely brilliant," a drunken English professor had said at a party some months before. "Never saw anything like it. Brilliant." Then, with a lurch and a hiccup: "For an undergraduate, of course.")

There would be no Phi Beta Kappa key; that 64 in calculus all those semesters ago had ensured that my four-year academic average would fall short of the required 88.

But in at least one way I had lived up to the example my brother had set: I had graduated with honors.

—————7—————

And so at the end of June 1962 I found myself behind the counter of the men's locker room at the Evanston Y, at the beck and call of any man or boy with a dime for a towel. It paid about 75 cents an hour, and it was the only part-time job I could find. Hardly an auspicious start for the career of a young man with a brand-new Bachelor of Arts degree.

But my shame soon faded. Evanston is a college town, and its Y employed graduate students in all sorts of jobs, from janitors to gym instructors, and the locker-room clientele knew it. A few ignorant souls might assume I was a towel boy because I could do nothing else, but the handball players who stopped by my counter included professors, lawyers, and businessmen, and they noticed and commented on the books I was reading during slow periods. Several even gave me genuine insights into them.

And, much to my surprise, I liked my

summer studies at the Medill School of Journalism. In the 1950s and 1960s, along with Columbia University and the University of Missouri, Medill was a member of the highest triumvirate of the nation's journalism schools. Unlike most other J-schools, which viewed themselves as scholarly institutions and emphasized research and theory, Medill was not at all academically pretentious. Its graduate program was in many ways as intellectually rigorous as any other academic department, but deep down Medill thought of itself as a trade school that produced journalistic craftsmen the way vocational schools turned out union-certified plumbers. Its aim was to teach students how to use pencil and typewriter the way carpenters wield hammer and saw: with care and precision and without a wasted movement. It succeeded so well that major metropolitan newspapers everywhere regarded its graduates as instantly employable, often hiring them right out of school instead of waiting for them to acquire a few years' seasoning on small-town dailies.

Some of Medill's professors were tenured, distinguished holders of doctorates who had earned their spurs in the field, but more were working journalists who labored full-time for Chicago newspapers and magazines. They

155

taught part-time at Medill for two reasons: to earn a few freelance dollars and because deep down in every good journalist a schoolmaster struggles to emerge. Many develop highly individualistic ways of working that they think worth passing on to a new generation.

Richard T. Stout was my first teacher at Medill. He later went on to national fame as a Washington correspondent and pundit, but in the early 1960s he was a general-assignment reporter for the Chicago *Daily News*. At Medill that summer, he taught a section of Beginning Reporting. It was one of the several undergraduate courses I had to take to fulfill the requirements for the master's degree program; Trinity had offered no journalism courses.

Tall, beetle-browed, blunt-spoken, and easy to lipread, Stout devoted part of every two-hour session to war stories of Chicago journalism—stories that had a sharp point. He'd use them, for example, to show how an enterprising reporter could score a beat ("scoop" was a 1920s cliché nobody used anymore) on a competitor. More important, he showed us how to assemble the facts of a story with precise and colorful thews and sinews. A news story, he pointed out, could be either informative and dull or informative and readable. A newspaper that had more of the latter than the former would also have more readers than its gray competitors. Here was no pale-palmed oracle from the ivory tower, but a battle-scarred veteran from the trenches. His course was a paradigm of applied intelligence.

Dick Stout corrected his students' stories in the same endearing way. They'd come back to us hen-tracked in red ink, our many errors highlighted with a scrawled "Oh, Jesus!" or "You gotta be kidding!" He was quick to praise, too; a shapely phrase brought a simple but bold "Good!" or "Nice!" If we offered a controversial idea, he'd either agree or disagree in a lengthy mini-essay, scrawled on the back of the page.

Once I quoted a remark from Michael Harrington's *The Other America,* a book on poverty that had recently been published and was destined to become a classic. Stout had just read it, too, and was so moved that on the back of my story he delivered himself of a long opinion that I still consider to be as perfect a book review as can be written in five hundred words.

There was also Beginning Photography, a simple technical course that taught me how to look at the things I was learning to write about. The Nikon single-lens reflex cameras so common in photojournalism today had just begun to appear on the American market, and we were still using two kinds of antiques. One was the classic old newspaper lensman's camera, the bulky Speed Graphic. It was loaded with four-by-five-inch cut film in clumsy holders that had to be slipped in and out of the camera for every picture, and ate expensive flashbulbs by the dozen. The other was the Rolleicord, a smaller camera that produced two-and-a-quarter-inch square negatives on roll film. The Rollei was a two-lens reflex the user had to hold at waist level while he peered down into its viewfinder. It was as slow and unwieldy as the Speed Graphic. Used skillfully, however, both cameras produced negatives far superior in sharpness and clarity to today's best 35 millimeter work.

Today's photojournalist, equipped with a motor-drive Nikon, zoom lens, and quick-change film backs, returns from an assignment with hundreds, even thousands of shots of his subject taken from different perspectives. At least one photograph is bound to be good enough to make it into print. In the early 1960s, however, our primitive hardware ordinarily gave us a handful of chances—sometimes only one—to get a publishable photograph, and we had to make the most of them.

I learned to watch carefully, trying to anticipate the best moment to place the viewfinder of the heavy Speed Graphic against my eye, yank out the film curtain, and press the shutter. To maximize my chances of getting a good shot, I learned to research a photo assignment before going out into the field. If a photographer knew what was likely to happen, he could wait for just the right moment: the visual heart of a news story, its most dramatic component.

I am still proud of one particular photograph I took with the Speed Graphic at a press conference in an Evanston hotel that summer of 1962. It captures the Reverend Martin Luther King, Jr., finger thrust gently at his audience but righteous fire in his eye. Sure, it was a lucky shot—but it was a shot whose likelihood I had increased in the Medill library, poring over news clippings and wire-service stories about Dr. King.

Of these practical journalism courses, the one that finally convinced me of David Botter's wisdom was Copyreading. I had thought newspaper copyreaders—or copy editors, as they're called today—sat quietly around a desk dotting "i"s, crossing "t"s, and writing simple headlines, that their job must be the easiest and most boring imaginable, while the reporters and photographers did all the glamorous work in the field. Nothing could have been further from the truth.

The copyreader, I was to learn, is a news story's last best hope before it is converted into type. Under deadline pressure, a reporter often can make mistakes, committing grammatical errors, misspelling names, and locating events at the wrong times and in the wrong places, even nonexistent ones. Sometimes salient facts are buried deep in a story instead of placed at or near the top, where they can be most quickly appreciated. City editors catch most of these bloopers, but they themselves work against the clock, and errors frequently sneak past. All these things are also true of wire-service copy, such as that from the Associated Press and United Press International, which is produced under the same pressure and is subject to the same errors.

Copyreaders, therefore, must be not only Mrs. Grundys of grammar and Dr. Johnsons of usage but also expert rewriters. They must also be walking, talking encyclopedias and gazetteers, born skeptics and fact hounds with curious, hard-to-please minds. They must also be quick at writing headlines, a tricky task that's a difficult literary form in itself. Just try rendering eight hundred words of news story into thirty characters of headline.

The buck stops at the copy desk; if an error should get through, the copyreader catches the most hell. A reporter may win a Pulitzer Prize for a story largely hammered into shape by a copyreader; the reporter gets the glory, the copyreader nothing. Good reporters are easy to find, but expert copyreaders are worth their weight in diamonds. That's why they're paid more than reporters.

Furthermore, copyreading (I would quickly discover) is a highly suitable career for a deaf person—provided, of course, that the many requirements for the job are met. Copyreaders rarely, if ever, use the telephone. They take orders orally, but the great bulk of their work is done in silent concentration. To the public, copyreading may not be a glamorous occupation, but it has satisfactions of its own: done right, it's a highly intellectual, demanding job, and one can make a comfortable living at it on a big-city newspaper. Copyreading can also be a springboard to other, more specialized tasks in journalism, but I would learn this later.

As the summer ended, I became a full-time student and quickly fulfilled the undergraduate requirements. I opted for the magazine rather than the newspaper sequence of courses, for two reasons: the former would train me in the arts of writing long, detailed articles and I would avoid having to take one component of the latter: Advanced Reporting, a course that required much use of the telephone. Otherwise the sequences were largely similar; in fact, newspaper majors often went to work for magazines, magazine majors for newspapers. It didn't matter. I was hooked on journalism. Finally I had discovered what I was fit to do.

At this time I decided to do something about my speech, which I thought might be beginning to deteriorate. It seemed that people were asking me more often to repeat what I had said. Five years had passed since I last had any sort of speech therapy, and perhaps it was time for a refresher course.

Northwestern seemed the perfect place for

it. The famous Institute of Language Disorders occupied a rundown war-surplus building just a hop and a skip upcampus from Fisk Hall, home of Medill. If I could get in a couple of sessions of speech therapy each week, I thought, perhaps the deterioration would halt and even could be reversed.

The institute of 1962 still subscribed to its academic philosophy of 1949: the psychology of the deaf was considered as important as the everyday tasks of auditory and speech pathology. Therefore, in order to take speech therapy, I would first have to submit to an all-day battery of tests designed to measure my intelligence and mental health, then hear the results in a "counseling session."

At this I balked. It was my speech I wanted help for, I protested, not my psyche. The institute's reply was that the data "would be used to help other deaf people." This, I suspected from my own studies of psychology at Trinity, ranked on the scale of veracity somewhere between "The check is in the mail" and "Your car will be ready by noon." I knew full well that the data would end up in a lonely file drawer, that the information was intended mainly to help an ambitious scholar earn a Ph.D. But I assented. It was the only way I could get help for my speech.

I had a chip on my shoulder the size of a shed roof. It had not been long since I had experienced an emotional crisis that was the direct result of my deafness, and I was still wary of those who might tell me that I could not do this or that because I was deaf. I had just discovered that my future lay in journalism, which educators of the deaf did not consider a promising field for the deaf because of their problems with language and communication. And I had just read a good deal of muckraking journalism about psychological testing abuses in the corporate world. It had outraged me. Clearly I was not the perfect subject for such testing. But the tester didn't know that.

Furthermore, at twenty-two I was still immature, both emotionally and intellectually. Possibly, but not necessarily, because I was deaf. It's said that the deaf tend to score lower on assessments of maturity than their hearing contemporaries, because difficulties in communication retard their social development. In my case heredity, that infamous Kisor slowness to mature, probably was as much to blame as environment for my callowness.

At the session's conclusion, the tester, an assistant professor of educational audiology I'll call Miss Jones, wanted my parents to hear the results. On the phone Mother declined to come in for a conference. "He is twenty-two years old," she said. "He is an adult. Tell him yourself. As for us, we are convinced he is going to achieve his goals, no matter what you say." Or words to that effect.

So I went in. Miss Jones told me what I expected she would. I needed speech therapy, and I also needed counseling over my future. Certainly I was intelligent and well educated, but I had to be more realistic about my goals—writing, editing, and teaching— and I had to learn to "accept my deafness." I was, she said, "denying" it by refusing to associate with my fellow deaf. This was not healthy. I should join a local organization for the deaf and learn something about deafness.

I don't recall exactly what I replied, but it must have had something to do with grandmothers and egg sucking. After a few inconclusive weeks of speech therapy with Miss Jones, during which she resolutely and repeatedly attempted to bring up the matter of counseling and I resolutely and repeatedly refused to listen, I simply stopped attending the sessions.

A few years later, using a common investigative ploy that every journalist would recognize but which I cannot reveal, I obtained a copy of the case history that Miss Jones had filed on me. Not long ago I dragged it out of dusty storage for a close examination. It is very revealing, both about me and about the educational establishment of the deaf of the times.

In many places I had a good laugh. Among the "indications" Miss Jones found were "homosexual tendencies" and a propensity for "adolescent sexual fantasy." The sole evidence for the former seemed to be that my interests tended toward the feminine because I scored high on literary and artistic tests and low on mechanical ones. Today that notion seems appallingly sexist and even homophobic. But Miss Jones came from the dominant culture, one that considered a strong interest in the arts to be weak and effeminate, one that believed it was unmanly to write about nuances of feeling with grace and delicacy.

As for the dirty-mindedness, of course I thought about sex all the time when I was twenty-two years old. Doesn't any healthy young man of that age, especially one who happens at the moment to be between—ahem!—heterosexual relationships? Nobody had asked me about those—just the cut-and-dried survey questions on the battery of tests.

But one of Miss Jones's conclusions simply puzzles me. "His fluent expression of written language," she wrote, "is interpreted by the tester as indicating that he finds trouble in relating to people." Does good writing necessarily imply misanthropy? Maybe it does, and if so, I'd like to know how. So, presumably, would a host of journalists and novelists and poets.

At least once, Miss Jones leaped to an utterly wrong-headed conclusion. I had written that a picture of several figures suggested Mother attempting to shush my five-year-old sister, Debbie, and her friends while I studied downstairs and "tried to ignore the clatter of little hoofs above." That last phrase indicated to Miss Jones that the subject might be "denying his acceptance of deafness and really wanting to hear." It did not seem to have occurred to her that deaf people, too, feel the vibrations of and are annoyed by the racket small children make.

Let alone that deaf writers, too, can essay aural metaphors as well as visual ones.

To be fair to her, I must admit that Miss Jones's conclusions were not entirely off base. Of course I was "hostile," and it's a pity Miss Jones had stuck to the battery of laboratory questions instead of attempting to elicit some information about the recent events in my life. As had her colleague Helmer Myklebust more than a decade before, she believed six hours of testing could illuminate all corners of a complex situation. Had she made some effort to observe my life outside her office, she might have interpreted some of her data in a different manner, and we might have enjoyed a little rapport.

As for the perceived "dislike of authority," Miss Jones was right, but she had no idea, I think, that this characteristic would be a help rather than a hindrance in my newly chosen profession. Of course, I didn't know it at the time either, but contempt for authority is considered a perfectly healthy, even desirable mind-set for a journalist.

I won't quibble, however, with Miss Jones's finding that I scored low on the social maturity scale, which measures an individual's ability to function among large numbers of people. Even more than a quarter of a century later I think I'd still bring up the caboose on such a test.

Nor can I take issue with Miss Jones's statement that I refused to associate with the deaf. To one of her questions I had written frankly that I stayed away from other deaf people because they behaved peculiarly, were too clannish, and depended too much on others for help. Associating with them, I feared, would diminish me in the eyes of hearing people. I did not think the limitations of the deaf in general applied to me, and I did not want the hearing to feel that they did, either. Miss Jones evidently believed that they did, or she would not be trying to dissuade me from my chosen career.

Did this mean, as Miss Jones thought, that I was "denying" my deafness? In a way she was right and in another she was wrong. It's true that I knew very little about other deaf people and indeed subscribed to the ordinary hearing person's stereotyped notions about them, simply because I was culturally a member of the hearing world.

Because I had always lived among the hearing, I had looked at deafness not as an existential condition to which I must submit—the view of most deaf people and professionals in the field—but as an adversary to defeat. Riding the tiger of deafness today seems just a vainglorious notion, the striking of a noble but doomed pose, like those pigeon-splattered statues of Confederate cavalrymen in the courthouse squares of so many Southern towns. Yet it was for an ambitious young deaf man a useful, workable idea, one that could keep him forging ahead until he had grown old enough to recognize his limitations and accept them with equanimity. And in the summer of 1962 I was actively fighting battles with my old enemy, losing some skirmishes but winning others. The campaign was still undecided, but I had gained a tactical advantage with my discovery at Medill that my future lay in journalism.

If I was uninformed about the larger world of the deaf, Miss Jones was equally uninformed about journalism. "The question of life goals should be examined closely by the patient over the next year," she wrote in dubious conclusion to her case history. But she was an audiologist, not a professor of communications, and knew only what her specialty had told her about the capabilities of her clients (that "patient" was a telling slip). How could she know what I knew about journalism? I had only just learned it myself.

Shortly before Thanksgiving 1962, I spotted a small card on the "Positions Available" bulletin board at Medill. A Chicago-based sailing magazine needed a temporary editorial assistant to help get out its special New Year's issue. The card, dusty and stained, must have languished on the board for weeks.

The holidays were approaching and, like most graduate students, I was nearly broke, despite my job at the Y. I asked Mother to call the number on the card and see whether the job was still open. I wasn't optimistic, but I had nothing to lose. As usual, Mother explained why I couldn't speak on the phone myself. The reply was curt but surprising: "I don't care if he's deaf. Can he write?"

Johnny Wilson, the harassed managing editor of *One-Design Yachtsman: The Magazine of Sailboat Racing,* was a rough-hewn former sportswriter from Miami. Short, stocky, crew-cut, and pockmarked, he looked a little like Mickey Spillane and spoke out of the side of his mouth the same way,

171

with a voice as melodious as a wheelbarrow of gravel bumping over cobblestones.

He knew nothing about deaf people. He had formed no prejudices about their capabilities, because he had never known, or heard about, any. And he was desperate. His was a fledgling magazine with a growing but still small circulation, and its wages were meager. Nobody seemed to want the job he was offering. He had decided he'd take the first warm body that walked into the office, so long as it knew how to assemble a sentence grammatically.

"Can he come down *today?*" he asked Mother. An hour later I was in his office. As we shook hands, his first words were: "Can you start now?" I could and did. The work was simple—a high school journalism student could have done it—but it was more interesting than pushing towels at the Y.

The January issue of the magazine was to contain a pictorial catalogue of more than five hundred racing sailboats, from eight-foot dinghies to the stately America's Cup twelve-meter yachts. Having "messed about in boats" at Camp Echo, I knew a little about the subject. It wasn't difficult to translate manufacturer's brochures into short paragraphs describing the length, beam, sail area, and other characteristics of each boat, with a sentence or two about the things that set it apart from other sailboats. In a few hours I had the task down to a formula, batting out a new paragraph every five minutes or so.

Wilson was delighted. When that job was completed a couple of weeks later, instead of giving me a check and a goodbye handshake, he thought I might continue to be useful if I could come in for a few hours a couple of times a week. He'd show me how to lay out and paste up page dummies of the catalogue from galley proofs of the paragraphs I had written, and how to read the page proofs when they arrived from the printer. This was hardly an unfamiliar task. It was the kind of thing I'd done as managing editor at Evanston High, and I took to it as swiftly as a swallow to the wind. Before long Johnny had me editing copy and writing headlines and helping plan the contents of the entire magazine.

"You've got talent, kid," he'd say after a day of hard work, and I'd beam with pleasure. I was on my way.

Partly to earn money for school and partly to gain the experience, I delayed my return to Medill for two quarters while working full-time for *One-Design Yachtsman*. Most of my tasks were purely editorial, but on two occasions Johnny sent me on the road to write articles about regattas. I'll never know for certain, but I think Johnny had two motives for doing so—first, to get more material for the magazine, and second, to see what my limitations as a reporter might be.

So long as I could talk to people face to face, I could get the information I needed for a story. These brief field trips, however, didn't involve telephone newsgathering, as does most professional reporting. If they were inconclusive in demonstrating my journalistic limitations, they did show me that I was happiest at an editor's desk. On the road, I often had to ask people to repeat what they'd said. As an editor I rarely had to do that, and my growing skills, at any rate, seemed most valuable at the desk.

Halfway through this period Johnny, sick unto death of Chicago winters, resigned to return to Florida. He had been a superb teacher, and had carved enough raw skill out of me so that for the next three months I could do most of the editorial and production work of the magazine almost alone under the sharp eye of Knowles Pittman, the publisher, as supportive in his quiet, intellectual way as Johnny had been in his craggy manner. I had needed a break, and Johnny and Knowles gave it to me in spades.

When I returned to Medill in the fall of 1963, I had an advantage over most of my classmates: the kind of experience and responsibility a young journalist doesn't ordinarily get until long after graduation. It stood me in particularly good stead in the Editorial Operations graduate course, in which the class of sixteen students was divided into two news desk staffs, each responsible for producing a mock newspaper during a three-hour lab. We'd rip copy from the Associated Press and United Press International teletypewriters, lay out pages, edit stories to fit their holes, and write headlines for them.

Johnny and Knowles had taught it all, the raw-copy-to-finished-product approach, and my performance impressed the course's instructor, Dan Sullivan, who was then cable editor of the Chicago *Daily News*—another major-league newspaperman moonlighting as a professor. "Sully," bespectacled, balding, and brush-cut, looked like a middle-aged nerd, complete with plastic pocket protector. He was an old-fashioned newspaperman's newspaperman, with an intense, inquiring, and retentive mind that knew no boundaries. And he was a patient, compassionate teacher, the kind who took a personal interest in his students. Near the end of the quarter he drew me aside and said quietly, "In a couple of years, come look me up."

This time, going through the job-interview mill was different. I knew that I had value as a journalist and—thanks to my experience at *One-Design Yachtsman*—knew exactly what it was. So long as I did not have to use the telephone, I could edit. I was good at taking a piece of raw, unruly copy and blue-penciling it to its essence, making sure of the facts as I went along, and searching out its heart for the headline. Sullivan said he thought I was a natural newspaper copyreader and, even if I still wanted to work on magazines someday, a few years of newspaper experience would stand me in good stead.

The interviews were hugely different from those at Trinity. My voice was no longer a nervous squeak, but strong, confident, and poised. I was proud of my résumé, which included straight A's at Medill and a sheaf of bylined clippings from *One-Design Yachtsman.*

And the employment market was wide

open. Not for a few years would journalism —still as low-paying as elementary school teaching—surge in popularity as a career after college. Like Johnny Wilson, newspaper recruiters were looking for warm bodies. Whatever unease my deafness raised in them apparently was overwhelmed by my thick résumé, which included recommendations from the part-time instructors—professional newsmen, not just teachers—attesting to my ability to do the copyreader's task as well as any hearing person.

Before graduation half a dozen offers came my way. The two most attractive were at the Denver *Post* and at the *Evening Journal* of Wilmington, Delaware. The latter (circulation 90,000) was small enough so that a new editor on its five-person news copy desk could quickly gain experience editing all kinds of articles, from local squibs to major breaking national and international news. And so, a week after receiving my MS in journalism degree with distinction as well as a couple of top-student awards, I piled my belongings into my Volkswagen and drove east. I was to be paid $87.50 a week—a munificent sum considering I had been making $75 a week at *One-Design Yachtsman*.

The day I arrived in Wilmington to look

for an apartment, the temperature was in the humid nineties. After studying the classified ads, I went to the city's largest real estate agency, thoroughly sweat-sodden in wrinkled, wilted shirt sleeves. When I told the receptionist that I was answering an ad for an apartment, she looked me up and down and turned to a manager at a desk nearby. I did not see what she said, but he looked me over and said, "I'm sorry, all our apartments have been rented."

Such was my naïveté that not for a long time did I realize I had gotten the brush-off. It could have been because I was deaf, therefore presumably unemployable and a poor risk for the rent. My scruffy appearance that sweltering day, however, probably would have scared away even the most enlightened apartment manager. I'll never know the truth.

That night I stayed in a motel. The next morning, dressed in coat and tie, I tried again, this time at the offices of a downtown dentist, who was advertising a $55-a-month walk-up efficiency apartment above a women's dress shop downtown, just three blocks from the *Evening Journal* plant. "I've just been hired as an editor at the paper," I said to introduce myself, and the apartment—

which had been vacant for many weeks—was mine. It was tiny and bare and, I am sure, quite depressing. The only furniture it ever held, aside from a bed and a bookcase, was an aluminum lawn chair. But it was *my* apartment. I was on my own—free, independent, and gainfully employed.

Professionally, the ten months I spent in Wilmington were highly valuable. At first the other members of the copy desk seemed wary, but after a few days they warmed up to me. Like any other young recruit, I was in the beginning given "shorts"—one-paragraph squibs—to edit. Then, as the "slot man"—as we called the copy chief, who sat in a niche at the center of a large semi-circular desk feeding raw copy to the editors on the "rim"—grew more confident in my talents, I was given more important work to do. In a few weeks I was handling my share of breaking news. At no time did the veterans patronize me as a deaf person, although I did come in for the usual gentle hazing every greenhorn had to suffer.

The only exasperation they ever displayed came during our lunch-hour bridge games. Despite their best efforts, I never could learn more than the rudiments of bridge, for I have absolutely no card sense. They shrug-

179

ged indulgently. "You can be dummy," they would say, and if the irony of that phrase ever occurred to them, they never acknowledged it.

Like young journalists everywhere, I wanted to do everything, to write as well as edit. A fellow editor, knowing of my wide reading interests, suggested I do as he did—write book reviews for the *Evening Journal*'s sister paper, the *Morning News*. There was no critic's fee—just the free copy of the book under review—but I loved reading novels and felt honored to render a printed judgment upon them. So enthusiastic was I that I suggested to the feature editor that perhaps I could review subtitled foreign films as well.

I was young enough and brash enough to think I could get away with it. As I had done in school, I prepared for the task by researching the film, reading criticisms of the director's previous films as well as magazine reviews of the one under notice. Wilmington was far enough off the first-run path so that national magazines and newspapers would carry their notices weeks before the movie arrived in town.

Half a dozen times this system worked well. But one night I got my comeuppance when an Italian movie featuring Sophia Loren arrived in town. It was the wrong print, with dubbed English instead of subtitles. I had little idea what was happening on the screen—it was a drama with a great deal of dialogue and little action—and when I wrote the review at the office that evening, I had to fake it. The resultant review was skewed enough from reality so that the sharp-eyed feature editor (who himself had seen the movie the same night) immediately spotted my little exercise in fraud. He suggested gently that it might be better for my moonlighting career if I stuck to book reviewing, and I had to agree.

Back to books it was, and by the spring of 1965 I had persuaded the editor of the *Evening Journal* to let me write a weekly literary column for the paper, focusing on local books and authors. I should have been content—my career was growing, and I was gaining respect as an up-and-coming young journalist around town. I was, however, beginning to chafe.

Wilmington may have been a fine place to work, but socially it was a wasteland. It was and is a company town; in the 1960s, if you did not work for Du Pont, you were nobody in white-collar society. The *News* and the *Journal* were owned by Du Pont, but their employees—especially the young ones—did not have the social cachet of those in the corporate mainstream. And if you weren't a member of the Wilmington Country Club, which was practically a Du Pont subsidiary, there wasn't much social life for you.

Hence I spent many of my weekends visiting friends in New York City and in Washington. There was an old girlfriend in Manhattan, but I was especially interested in a Northwestern classmate who had joined the faculty at the University of Virginia in Charlottesville. Sharon was a Kentuckian, a cute little slip of a thing barely five feet tall from Louisville who had graduated from the University of Kentucky. A former cheerleader, she was perky and bright though not an intellectual. Like Rachel, however, she was warm, open, and curious about everything. And, like Rachel, she was a product of her prefeminist times, perhaps more alert for marriage prospects than career opportunities.

From the first we got along like puppies. Sharon's casual Kentucky drawl was easy to lipread, and she understood my speech readily. As a Southerner, I think, she had learned to tolerate a wider range of human vagaries, including speech patterns, than most Northerners had. Southerners, in my experience, are more easygoing and patient with people whose behaviors differ from the norm. Why, I don't know. It may have to do with the slower, perhaps less judgmental pace of life below the Mason-Dixon Line.

It was clear from the beginning, however, that Sharon was much more interested in large social groups than I was. She had been the belle of many balls in Kentucky and loved to dress up and go to gatherings that attracted lots of other dressed-up people. Dutifully, I let Sharon drag me to them, though given my druthers I'd have gone someplace else.

At this time, I was starting to learn, perhaps unconsciously, that I functioned best in small groups, not at large parties. The problem didn't lie so much in lipreading; people in large gatherings tend to congregate in small conversational knots that are easy enough for a lipreader to cope with. The difficulty was in making myself understood. Though it is intelligible in a quiet room, my low, nasal, breathy deaf speech easily gets lost in a forest of competing voices. My most troublesome sounds—the fricatives "th," "f," and "s" and the long vowels "a" and "e"—are often too diffuse to be discerned against a noisy background. And when I raise the volume of my voice, the sounds tend to grow even more distorted. The noisier the party, the harder it is to understand my speech.

And so I'd stand silently at Sharon's elbow, smiling and nodding as she chattered on. That was all right with me. She talked enough for both of us.

Before this problem could come to a head, however, we had graduated and scattered to our new jobs. Sharon was four hours from Wilmington by car, and in the beginning I'd drive down almost every weekend to visit her in either Washington or Charlottesville. But time and distance inevitably take a toll on every relationship, and one day I received a letter from Sharon telling me, gently but clearly, that there was someone else in her life.

It was just as well. As a Southerner, Sharon was a churchgoing, Bible-reading evangelical Christian with a decent respect for virginity, and I a Northern agnostic with small sympathy for either organized religion or traditional sexual codes. That, I am certain, contributed more to the breakup of our relationship than my deafness.

My heart was again broken, although I had been slowly growing aware that our differences spelled doom for our affair. It is always better to be dumper than dumpee, and this was the second time I had been handed my walking papers. There was a difference, however: I had not been rejected because I was deaf. There followed a decent period of mourning, then a return to circulation.

Without an out-of-town girlfriend to go visit, I had to fend for myself in Wilmington. There was a popular bar near my apartment that attracted young downtowners after work—you might call it a rudimentary singles bar, but it was a quiet place, not a noisy circus like modern "meat markets." There I met two young secretaries and dated them casually for several months. It was then that a special problem of the young deaf adult who lived alone began to emerge: the inability to use a telephone.

For a long time, when I was in high school, I had to ask my friends or Mother or Dad (Buck was off at college) to call my girlfriends to set up dates. This is no way to conduct a love life, having your *mother* ask if so-and-so would like to go to the movies, or maybe to Wimpy's for a shake, or whatever. Mine was very good about it, because there was nothing else to be done. She and I both had to grit our teeth and be brave. I am sure she was as relieved as I when Debbie grew large enough to hold a telephone handset. There is something wonderfully conspiratorial between a big brother and a little sister in matters of the heart. During the two years I lived at home while attending Medill, Debbie served as a very efficient social secretary, not only calling dates but reminding me when it was time to go out on them.

But I was in Wilmington and she in Evanston. So long as I weekended out of town, I could write letters to set up dates. But without somebody—parent, sibling, friend, roommate—to serve as my telephone mouthpiece, carrying on an ordinary social life in Wilmington was cumbersome. Making dates there required quick footwork at the mailbox. Letters would have to be mailed by Tuesday if a reply was to come by Thursday or Friday, too late to recoup the weekend if my proposal was turned down. Before long I refined the method. I'd be my own mailman, delivering the messages around Wilmington myself, dropping them off in the morning on the way to work and picking up the replies sometimes that evening, sometimes the following morning. The young women I dated in this way were perfectly understanding, if a bit amused by my one-man Pony Express.

They were not entertained, however, when I tried to save a few hours by ringing their doorbells to negotiate the time for a date face to face. Several times a prospective date greeted me in curlers, face cream, and dismay, and I'm certain that on at least one occasion I interrupted something passionate. Urban Americans do not drop in unannounced at each other's homes.

Local dates thus became a sometime thing, and as my out-of-town relationships waned, I began to spend a lot of lonely evenings in Wilmington. Like so many young adults in a strange city, I began to think about home. A host of friends remained in Chicago; would I be happier in my old hometown?

I wrote to Dan Sullivan, who, as good fortune had it, was now copy desk chief of the Chicago *Daily News*. Were there any openings? Yes, there were, and the fellow who did the hiring immediately telegraphed me with a job offer. He was Creed Black, the managing editor, who coincidentally had resigned as editor of the Wilmington papers just before my arrival, in a dispute with the owners over how news affecting Du Pont should be played in its newspapers.

Sullivan sent me a copy of the memo of recommendation he had given Black. "Henry is one of the five or six best students I've had over the years," he had said. "At Medill he held his own in the daily copy-desk repartee," he added, referring to the mostly genial, sometimes sharp-edged abuse copyreaders liked to heap upon each other during slow moments. This was the sole reference in that memo he made to my deafness, and it was an oblique one. Even after a quarter of a century in journalistic harness, I've received few encomiums I'm as proud of as that one.

I was now in the big time as a staff member of a major metropolitan newspaper, and a distinguished one at that. The *Daily News*, more than a century old, had fielded the world's first foreign service and was still known as a writer's newspaper, favoring good prose as well as distinctive reporting. Its veteran correspondents were nationally famous, thanks to the joint news service the

Daily News put out with its sister morning newspaper, the Chicago *Sun-Times*.

But like big-city evening newspapers everywhere in America, it was losing circulation, owing to the inroads of the 5 p.m. television news and the difficulties of trucking newspapers from the presses to the suburbs on crowded daytime expressways. The moment I sat down for the first time on the rim of the *Daily News* copy desk in May 1965, a white-haired veteran peered from under his green eyeshade, shook my hand gravely, and said, "You're making a mistake, kid. This paper is about to fold." A dozen years would pass before his forecast came true, and they would be among the best of my life.

——8——

Almost as soon as I set up housekeeping in my new apartment in a high-rise building on Chicago's Near North Side, I obtained a hearing-ear cat. Well, sort of.

Fred was a large yellow tom of vague ancestry. I didn't acquire him expressly as a guide cat; felines are too independent, arrogant, and ornery to be educated about such things. He just arrived one day, an ineffably cute stray kitten, the gift of someone on a floor below who had found him wandering the plaza in front of our building. But Fred had his moments.

Whenever anyone knocked on the door of my efficiency apartment, he'd sit up straight and stare at the door. A second knock and he'd run to the door as if expecting the friendly fishmonger. I'd spot his movements and open the door myself. This worked about 90 percent of the time, so long as I was awake.

At other times Fred could be a hazard.

One evening as I slept, he padded in the dark atop the bookcase next to my bed and knocked over my alarm clock. The clock, a popular hardware-store item sold to people who hated noisy alarms, featured a lamp that flashed on and off repeatedly for a minute or two before triggering an audible alarm. It fell on its back, pressing in the plunger that stilled both alarms. As a result, I was two hours late at the *Daily News,* where I worked the midnight-to-8 a.m. shift.

Fred was by no means stupid. While still a kitten he learned that when I was asleep, yowling for his dinner fell on deaf ears, and that only when my eyes were open could he expect me to open the pantry door, too. So he'd roust me out by sitting on my chest and sandpapering my eyelids with his tongue. That is hardly a pleasant way to awaken.

Worse—for him—he seemed to think all humans were deaf, just as I thought, when I was a toddler, that everybody read lips. While still a stripling Fred tried the eyelid-grinding gambit on Craig, a Harvard Law School student who briefly shared my apartment that first summer. Craig awoke with a pained cry and with a reflexive sweep of his hand rocketed Fred across the bed and into the wall. The thump addled Fred's person-

191

ality, and for the rest of his short life he behaved in unpredictable and neurotic ways.

These days hearing-ear dogs for the deaf are common. Though of course I can't take credit for it, perhaps I was the first to conceive of the idea, when I was about sixteen. Shortly after dawn one brisk spring Sunday I had driven the family collie to the public beach in neighboring Wilmette for a run. I'd thought that no policeman would be around at that early hour to enforce the "No Dogs" sign at the entry to the park.

But no. Within ten minutes a prowl car had parked and an elderly cop trudged through the sand to the water's edge where the boy and his dog sat, the picture of innocent togetherness. "Didn't you see that sign, sonny?" he growled, upholstering his ticket book. He had the drop on me. "Yes, Officer," I said, thinking fast, "but you see I'm deaf, and my dog is a hearing-ear dog. You know, like a seeing-eye dog for blind people."

The policeman gazed at the collie, which by now had trotted a hundred yards up the beach and was sniffing happily at a dead fish, oblivious to the world. Lifting one eyebrow in disdain, the policeman said, "Your driver's license, please."

Clearly the hearing-ear dog was an idea whose time had not yet come, and the fine was five dollars.

But now the time had come for other ideas. Ever since I had retired my squealing hearing aid at age ten, I had not used any kind of artificial device to make up for my deafness. None had seemed necessary, and in any event I knew of none. I could always depend on hearing people to make phone calls or answer the doorbell. But now that I was a bachelor living solo in a high rise, with friends to come calling, it was clear I needed help. Fred notwithstanding, I had to be able to know when someone was buzzing my apartment from the foyer many floors below, so that I in turn could press a button to let the caller into the building.

My old chum Sam Williamson, now a brand-new Ph.D. in economics and an instructor at the University of Iowa, had the answer. Since boyhood he had been an electronics hobbyist, the sort of inspired tinkerer who could build a shortwave radio out of bell wire and bottle caps. One day, when he paid a visit to my apartment, I laid the problem before him. He thought for a moment, then borrowed a screwdriver and removed the grille that concealed the apartment's intercom system. He poked about inside, nodded sagely, then said he'd be back the next weekend with something that ought to work.

He returned with a crude wooden box painted black, several wires hanging from its innards. Inside lay a spaghetti maze of wire and switches. Sam placed the box on a table underneath the grille, wrapped the bare ends of two slim wires around terminals on the buzzer, then plugged a common household electrical cord into a 115-volt outlet in the wall. Instantly I saw the principle, which sounds complicated but is really very simple.

When someone far below pressed the annunciator button, the buzzer's six-volt current would trip a low-voltage relay switch. That in turn would trip another relay, a bigger one. The large relay switch would close a second circuit. At one end of the second circuit was the electrical cord and plug for the 115-volt house current. At the other end was a receptacle into which Sam plugged an ordinary table lamp. Inside the lamp's electrical socket Sam placed a thin metal wafer, a common dime-store device that causes a light bulb to flash constantly.

So long as someone below leaned on the buzzer button, the lamp would flash. As

194

soon as the button was released, the lamp would stop flashing. What a devilishly simple idea! I pumped Sam's hand, thanked him profusely, and blessed him and all his children and grandchildren to come.

Today Sam's black box seems embarrassingly primitive. A good-sized hardware store might be stocked with scores of electronic "assistive devices" now available for the hearing-impaired. No deaf parents of a newborn, for instance, would be without a "baby crier," a microphone affixed to a crib that flashes a lamp when the infant wails. Or other such electronic visual attention getters as burglar alarms, wake-up alarms, fire and smoke alarms, pagers, phone and doorbell signalers, and more. Some of them, like Sam's gadget, operate ordinary household lamps. Others use strobe devices that look like electronic camera flashes but pack the power of stun grenades. Bed shakers, rough cousins of motel-room Magic Fingers massagers, awaken exceptionally sound sleepers. These devices were a long time coming— many of them had to wait for the invention of the transistor—but when they finally began to appear, they made the lives of deaf people immeasurably easier. Including mine.

The telephone is probably the world's most unremarked appliance; once installed, it hardly earns a second thought in the hearing household. Telephone amplifiers for the hard-of-hearing have been around for a long time, but the deaf had no means of communicating on the phone until the late 1950s, when a deaf Bell Telephone engineer finally had a bright idea that solved the problem for some hearing-impaired people. He invented a device that would allow old wire-service teletype machines with keyboards to be plugged into ordinary voice telephone lines so that they could "speak" to each other. On one machine a deaf person typed out a message that was instantly transmitted to another teletype, which tapped it out onto a roll of paper. Thus was born the "TTY," as the deaf world calls the teletypewriter.

For those who could afford one, the TTY was a salvation from telephone isolation, but it had its drawbacks. Teletype machines were big, ugly, and rackety—not that the noise disturbed their owners. And a TTY user could (and still can) talk only to another person owning a similar device.

The closed world of the deaf grew larger, but it remained circumscribed, for TTYs were to be found only among deaf people and their organizations. As I grew into young manhood, I often wished I owned a TTY, but inasmuch as all my friends and family were hearing, the idea of having such a device seemed an exercise in listening to the sound of one hand clapping.

That is, until the Sensicall came along in 1966, not long after Sam bestowed his magic set of relays upon me. It was a simple device cobbled together by a Western Electric telephone engineer and rented for a nominal sum by Illinois Bell. Nothing more than a small black box that plugged into an ordinary telephone, it bore a tiny red lamp that flashed on and off in time with the voice of the person calling. The idea was for a deaf person to watch the red lamp blink in Morse code as a hearing caller voiced the code orally with short "di"s and long "dah"s. With pencil and paper the deaf user could then decode the message—on the fly, if he knew Morse—and answer by speaking normally into the receiver.

This was a godsend. Only one of these devices was necessary—at my end. I could call perfect strangers, explain with speech that I was deaf but used a flashing lamp device that would respond to the oral noises they made. They might not know Morse code, I would say, but I'd ask simple yes-and-no questions that they could answer with a short "di" for "yes" or a long "dah" for "no," and I'd watch the flashing lamp and understand them that way.

This notion worked better in theory than it did in practice. For technical reasons my breathy speech does not come across well over the phone, unless the listener is accustomed to it. And almost always, a hearing person, confronted on the phone by a peculiar-sounding stranger with an outlandish proposal about flashing lights and "di"s and "dah"s, would be thoroughly nonplussed. Usually he'd hang up before I had a chance to finish my spiel. Clearly this idea needed more work.

Yet once my family and friends were "trained" in Morse—the process consisted of handing them small wallet-sized cards printed with the code—I could "talk" with them. Slowly and clumsily, yes, for the caller had to search out on the code card each combination of sounds that made up a letter of the alphabet, then sound it out into the telephone mouthpiece. Things stopped while I decoded each letter, then asked for the next one. The caller had to voice each sound crisply; drawling or huskiness often caused the lamp at my end to flicker crazily.

But the Sensicall was better than nothing. As Dr. Johnson observed about a dog's walking on its hind legs, one marveled not that it was done well but that it was done at all. And at last I had something with which I could talk to young women on the telephone without a go-between.

Good things, they say, come in threes. That same summer of Sam's gadget and the Sensicall, I met Debby.

She says that the idea of going out with a deaf man on a blind date almost overwhelmed her, and her roommate had to push her down the stairs to meet me. She says that she could not understand a word I said the entire evening. She says that before I had taken her home she knew she was going to marry me. Go figure.

With the ineffable wisdom of a young deaf bon vivant, I took Debby on that first date to a trendy cocktail lounge where for the entire evening my voice was drowned out by a bush-league Bobby Short at the piano. Debby says she was too frightened to tell me she couldn't hear me, let alone understand me.

But I didn't have any trouble lipreading Deborah Lee Abbott, a pretty young woman with the world's most adorable nose, eyes that still can mesmerize, an extraordinarily vivacious personality, and a sangfroid so unshakable that I had no idea she felt spooked on that blind date. We had been fixed up by an old girlfriend of mine, a fellow senior with Debby at National College of Education in Evanston.

As the pianist crashed out chords a few feet from our table, she told me that just two months earlier she had transferred from William Smith College in Geneva, New York, so that she could get a head start on a career as an elementary school teacher. She was from Marshfield in central Wisconsin, her engineer father owned a construction company, and her mother wrote and published children's stories. And she hoped to follow in her mother's footsteps.

"Ah, a fellow writer. This young lady is worth further investigation," I thought as I returned her to her hotel late that evening and said good night. A few days later I asked my friend Myron, a fellow copyreader at the *Daily News*, to call her and ask if she was free for dinner that Saturday night. She was sorry, she said, but she had made previous plans.

As Myron hung up, I said resignedly, "Oh, well, it was worth a try," and muttered something about other fish in the sea.

"Nononono, Henry," said Myron. "She *really* is interested. Try her again." Flies don't grow on Myron, who is a truly perceptive human being. He could hear the genuine regret in Debby's voice; her "I'd love to, but" was not a brush-off. A few days later I called her again, and she said yes. I'll save an entire chapter of this book simply by writing that one thing led to another, and another, and another. Some things are too precious not to keep private.

Debby says that what initially attracted her to me was that I was "interesting," clearly not one of what she considered a herd of "superficial" young careerists. The deafness, of course, was a novelty, part of the intrigue. In the beginning, she admits, she was a little disconcerted about the consequences of my speech in potentially awkward situations, such as ordering a meal in a noisy restaurant. (I simply have to repeat myself, sometimes with the help of a finger pointing at the item on the menu, until the waiter gets it right.) Once the newness wore off, she realized that we had a good deal in common: similar middle-class backgrounds, similar liberal politics, similar conservative views of family life.

She adds that we shared enough commonality so that she could shrug off, and even chuckle about, the genuinely embarrassing social situations into which my deafness sometimes lands me. One evening early in our courtship, we stopped in with friends at a popular Chicago folk music night spot. Of course, I wasn't interested in folk music, or music of any kind, but, deaf or not, one is smart to go with the social flow, and Debby wanted to hear the featured singer. I have no idea who that was, but she evidently sang like an angel, her heavenly voice warming the poorly heated club and moving the audience almost to tears. Except me.

As the last strains of the music drifted into the rafters and a hush settled over the club, I turned, shivering, to Debby. I had absolutely no idea that the song had ended and, in what must have been a reverent, even sepulchral silence, I loudly and clearly said, "Let's go. My ass is freezing off."

Ours was the first (and only) romance I have ever carried on via the telephone. You can guess what our conversations with the

Sensicall must have been like. In the beginning Debby sent each hard-earned endearment in painstakingly "tapped" Morse, and I'd reply with the usual sweetnesses in voice.

Before long we settled on a simple and quick way to chat: I'd do all the talking (the only time in our relationship I have ever been able to do so), and Debby would reply with "di" for "yes" or "dah" for "no" as appropriate. It was a ridiculously one-sided way to converse, but it sufficed.

What must strangers have thought when they happened upon a pretty young woman trilling "di-di dah-dah" nonsense into the receiver of a public pay phone? The scene might seem comic, but for me it meant a kind of rebirth.

Two decades ago Sam's box and the Sensicall seemed to me merely conveniences, like refrigerators and washing machines. They were marvelous gadgets, and I thought I'd miss them if they weren't around but I could live without them, as I had all my life. Of course, I missed the point. Modern conveniences are instruments of freedom. A life without something to cool perishables and freshen clothing would be a very different one. We would need to devote a great deal of time and energy to basic survival tasks such as obtaining fresh food and clean clothes. Life without fridges and washers would be tolerable, but our spheres of activity would be severely limited. We would have less freedom to do things that matter —such as communicating with the rest of the world.

Now it seems that, crude as those two early devices were, they meant the beginning of the end of my isolation—isolation from other people. Those who hear cannot imagine how grindingly lonely deafness often can be. A comfortable home can feel like a maximum-security prison if there is no easy means of communication with the outside. This is one important reason why the deaf tend to gravitate toward one another. Just as do the hearing, the deaf need to communicate, to share their thoughts and feelings with others. Only a fellow lifer in the jailhouse of silence understands how important that is to sanity and how difficult it can be to achieve.

Yes, I was living in the world of the hearing, and so long as I was in the presence of family, friends, and fellow workers, I connected. But I needed to enlarge the envelope of my life. As I grew older, like every other young man I needed to create and maintain my own physical and temporal space and from it communicate with the outside.

Partly because I now had a means of doing so, however crude it might be, my romance with Debby was of an entirely new kind. Every evening, not every other weekend, we communicated on the Sensicall and shared the day's events. Three or four times a week I'd call and say, "Have you got a bit of time before I go to work?" and forty-five minutes later, I'd be on her doorstep. Now I could act on impulse, just like everyone else. I didn't have to save my thoughts for days, waiting for the next time we met to spring them upon her.

Because we could now communicate so easily, our relationship was much more like those between hearing people, the kind of liaison I had not truly enjoyed with Rachel and Sharon. On my part at least, those relationships had involved a good deal of impatience. Communications when we were apart were slow and inefficient. When we were together, I was jealous of their time and attention. I wanted to be alone with them, to shut out the world, to have them all to myself. When I was not with them, I was also jealous—of the time and attention I knew other people must be enjoying with them. Including other men—*hearing* men, against whom I felt I could not compete. But now, at twenty-six, I was finally beginning to mature.

Debby's parents spend their summers in the Upper Peninsula of Michigan, on the southern shore of Lake Superior. Depending on the lake level, their cabin is twenty to fifty feet from the edge of the cold, clear, clean water. Every morning loons paddle by, and in season Canada geese tarry on their way south. This is wild, remote, lonely, and beautiful country, timbered out by the 1930s and now well into second-stage regrowth. Deer, raccoons, porcupines, and foxes abound, and black bears are returning to the lowlands from exile in the nearby Porcupine Mountains.

That was where I met Betty and Clark Abbott. At first they seemed bemused by the deaf young man their daughter had brought to their summer home. I knew it was up to me to cross the bridge, to meet them halfway, to show them that I was as normal and ordinary a young man as any Debby had dated. Fortunately the task was made easier because we had a good deal to talk about. I have no talent for comfortable small talk, the kind that helps create relationships. For me, communication with strangers is too difficult to waste on social noise.

Betty and Clark are well-informed, politically conscious, and socially concerned people who form reasoned opinions about national and world events. A young newspaperman's kind of people. At first our conversations were halting, but during the long, slow, cool weekend in that quiet cabin on the lakeshore, we started to become accustomed to one another's speech.

Betty and I both were voracious readers, and we talked about books. Clark and I exchanged opinions about the growing civil rights movement in the South. To my surprise the Abbotts, who lived smack in the middle of lily-white Republican country in central Wisconsin, were thumpingly in favor of the goals of A. Philip Randolph and Martin Luther King. I also learned that in the early 1950s the Abbotts had been all but ostracized in Marshfield for their vocal opposition to the depredations of Senator Joe McCarthy, the anti-Communist witch-hunter from Wisconsin.

This, I thought, was where Debby got her intelligent, open-minded character, her con-

science, her compassion, her selflessness—
the things I loved her for. After that Labor
Day weekend in the north woods, I began
to think that this was a family I might marry
into.

Shortly before her twenty-second birthday
that October, to my surprise as much as hers
I popped the question. She quietly put her
hand on mine and said yes.

Now began the complicated social maneu-
vers all young couples must endure to secure
the approval of both sets of parents to the
union. Mine seemed to think it a good
match. They had never expected their son
to marry any but a hearing woman, and they
liked Debby. The only one in my family who
disapproved was my little sister, Debbie,
who displayed the normal thirteen-year-old
girl's outrage that another woman—let alone
one with the same name—would come between her and her beloved big brother. (Yes,
the similarity in names did cause a few amusing problems later on. When Debby and I
visited my parents while Debbie was still
living with them, there was often confusion
when a boyfriend called for Debbie, but
Debby answered the phone. "Which one?"
she'd try to say as quickly as possible. Often
she couldn't cut in until the boy had un-

loaded several embarrassingly intimate endearments upon her.)

Betty Abbott, who had seen us come in from long walks on the Lake Superior shore, our arms entwined affectionately, knew that her youngest daughter had at last found the man with whom she would spend the rest of her life. All mothers have that sort of intuition, or maybe it's just a perceptive fatalism. "I hope you like Henry," she told Clark, "because I know Debby's going to marry him." He chuckled and dismissed the idea.

But, as did Spencer Tracy in the classic movie comedy *Guess Who's Coming to Dinner?* when Katharine Houghton announced that she was going to marry Sidney Poitier, Clark Abbott faced another test of character. I wrote him an old-fashioned letter telling him that Debby and I were in love and planned to marry, and hoped that he would give the union his blessing.

Immediately he telephoned his daughter. She wasn't going to marry me in some misguided act of compassion, he declared. Absolutely not. Did she really want to spend the rest of her life with a deaf man? Yes, she did, she said firmly.

It must have been wrenching for Clark. Debby was the baby of the family, the youngest of four children, the last to leave the nest. And for an uncertain existence with a physically handicapped young man? Yes, he was gainfully employed, but what were his prospects for the future?

But like her father, Debby had a strong will of her own, and Clark knew better than to try to turn her against her decision. Difficult as it may have been, Clark gave us his blessing. The Abbotts agreed to announce the engagement at a small party at their house in Marshfield during the Christmas holidays.

While all this was happening, I was utterly unaware of the behind-the-scenes drama, either before or after the die was cast. Clark was too much a gentleman, and too good a student of human nature, to attempt to dissuade me from marrying his daughter. Until Christmas the Abbotts maintained a discreet silence on the matter. So discreet, in fact, that they did not tell their other children that the man Debby was marrying was deaf. Debby's brother Bruce, who worked in the family firm, sensed his father's dismay. One day he looked across the office at his father and said, "Dad, we know something's wrong with Henry. Is he a Negro?"

Both Clark and Betty would have been

even more concerned had they known that the divorce rate of deaf-and-hearing marriages is close to 90 percent. Such marriages tend to break down for the usual reasons: because of a lack of understanding, communication, and flexibility between the partners. They are almost doomed from the outset because the partners belong to two vastly different cultures, the hearing and the deaf. It's extraordinarily difficult for two such people to bridge the deep cultural gulf between them. The chasm can be as vast as that between, say, a highly educated New York Fashion designer with sophisticated, liberal tastes and a blue-collar small-town manual laborer with an eighth-grade education and old-fashioned views of marriage.

But Debby and I were members of the same culture, the hearing culture. True, in some ways I might be an outsider, but not in those that mattered. We could bridge our differences as well as any other couple—perhaps better than some. For Debby is at the same time flexible and tenacious, with an exquisite sense of compromise yet a determination to hold her ground when she knows she is right. She was and is very skillful at levering a rigid, stubborn fellow like me into appreciating her point of view.

On June 24, 1967, we were married, and we have been together ever since.

In the beginning, my working habits were not exactly ideal for a brand-new marriage. The midnight-to-8 a.m. shift at the *Daily News* meant that I'd come home to our apartment in La Grange Park just after Debby had gone to her fifth-grade classroom at the elementary school up the street. I couldn't fall asleep until after noon, and wouldn't awaken till about 9 p.m., just before she went to bed. We enjoyed the resilience of youth, however, and made the most of our brief evenings as well as the weekends.

Most of the night owls on the graveyard shift on a major metropolitan newspaper were young editors and reporters with too little seniority to choose daytime slots. Others, especially those with children in college, needed the 10 percent night-shift differential in salary. A few were misfits who liked the solitude of the wee hours. And more than one used the shift as an escape from a difficult marriage.

But the work on the Blue Streak, the first of the six editions of the day, was fascinating. Most of the local copy had already been handled by the 4 p.m.-to-midnight shift, and the bulk of the stories that crossed the copy desk consisted of dispatches from the wire services and the Washington and foreign bureaus of the *Daily News*. The night copy chief, Bill Rising, a sandpapery, much-married old curmudgeon, had at first mightily resisted the assignment of a deaf editor to his shift. But he had no choice, and before long he realized that I knew my stuff.

Bill was not very easy to get along with. He hated to have his judgments contradicted, and he was prone to spout superannuated aphorisms of journalism, such as "Never write a headline longer than a newsboy can shout!" It did not seem to have occurred to him that newsboys shouted no more. But if he liked the work of an inexperienced editor, he'd dole out as much responsibility as he thought the youngster could handle.

Soon, on slow nights I'd sit in the slot, handing out copy and checking the work of other editors while Bill snoozed away on the rim. He trusted my judgment enough so that shortly after 5:30 a.m. one day in 1966, when the news came in from police headquarters that eight young nurses had been found murdered in a blood-spattered South Side flat, he told me to brace myself. I'd help handle the story, doing the sidebars while a veteran edited the main piece.

The news was so stunning that the editor in charge of the Blue Streak was momentarily dumbfounded, wondering out loud whether he should discard his plans for Page One, at that moment being assembled in the composing room one floor below. Bill had both the presence of mind and the temerity to spin around in his chair and bellow at his superior, "You're gonna rip that page apart. This is a big one!"

It was a baptism of fire, assembling "take" after "take" from the city desk, making sure that there were no contradictions, that all the important facts stood high in the story, and writing the headlines with only minutes to spare. The pressure was on, but we made our 7:10 a.m. press deadline with good, solid stories. Richard Speck may have been a heinous killer, but I owe him a debt of sorts: he helped me prove my competence. That may sound obscene, but it was a fact of the profession of journalism, at least before the explosion in specialization that began about 1980, that career advancement depended on timely and lively handling of crime and catastrophe. Only after paying our dues in the trenches of police news were we able to struggle out of them.

As time went on, I soon began working other jobs on the shift. When the night national and foreign editor was off duty, I'd fill in. This was fascinating, exacting work. Copy constantly flowed in from the clattering teletype machines in the wire room, bearing London, Paris, and Moscow datelines. Often I'd compile a single story with information from three different sources—the Associated Press, United Press International, and the *Daily News's* own correspondents. Once in a long while there'd be a discrepancy I couldn't solve on my own, and I'd ask someone on the copy desk to call the bureau or news service to check. My deafness never seemed a hindrance in this sort of work.

There was a telephone at the copy desk, and it was fairly busy during the last hour before Page One, the last to be sent to press, was "locked up" on the composing-room floor. These were the last years of "hot type," when pages were assembled in large steel forms from long "sticks" of soft metal type set and cast on Linotype machines. For the most part makeup editors could trim and adjust stories to fit their allotted holes, but as the deadline crept near, especially if there was breaking news, they'd phone the copy desk for aid. If I was in the slot, an editor on the rim would take the call and pass on the requests from below.

I never, however, worked the slot on really busy nights when Bill Rising was on duty—when there was a storm at sea, he commanded from the bridge—so I was never tripped up by the telephone under pressure. Had I remained on the night shift, I probably could have grown into a decent copy chief. But there was another problem, and it had nothing to do with my deafness. Despite working for two and a half years on the Blue Streak shift, I never was able to adjust my circadian rhythm so that I could consistently get eight hours of sleep each day. I was simply not a born night worker. During the day I'd toss and turn fitfully, getting less and less sleep as the week wore on, and make up for the deprivation by sleeping at night during weekends. Toward the end I became dependent on Placidyl, a sleeping drug that when abused causes the user to stumble around in a zombie-like fog, never quite fully alert.

I asked Dan Sullivan if he could assign me to the day shift. By then I had earned enough seniority to claim a daytime spot on the copy desk, and I slid into it gratefully. After ten days of cold-turkey withdrawal, I beat the Placidyl dependency and settled down to a more normal existence.

By this time, our son Colin was on the way. He was born September 18, 1969, at Evanston Hospital. In those days expectant fathers still waited offstage instead of playing a supporting role at the delivery, and I smoked cigarette after cigarette in the waiting room while Debby went through the last stages of labor.

Then the door opened and the obstetrician strode in. I recall that he looked tired and drawn, but assumed that that was normal for doctors called out of bed in the small hours. He smiled and shook my hand. "Congratulations," he said. "You have a son." I was so flooded with relief that I began trembling. "Thank you, Doctor," I said with a quaver in my voice. "Is everything all right?" Momentarily, he glanced away, then looked back at me. "Yes," he said. "Both Debby and the baby are well. You can go see them now."

Overwhelmed, I rushed into the recovery room. Debby was groggy, almost incoherent, unsmiling. The baby was not with her. "Let me sleep," she said irritatedly. A nurse brought Colin over and I held him briefly, tears in my eyes. Then I dashed to my parents' house to spread the good news.

The next day, recovered, Debby told me what had happened, what the obstetrician had concealed. Right after the moment of birth, she had suffered a grand mal seizure. The doctor had decided not to tell me. He didn't know whether I was capable, at that moment, of dealing with the news, what consequence my deafness might have, whether he could get across to me what the seizure meant. There are a number of causes of seizures during delivery, and one of the most common is a brain tumor. He felt he didn't need a second crisis on his hands.

It turned out that Debby did not have a tumor. We never learned what caused the seizure, although a neurologist later speculated that the cause might have been a chemical imbalance during pregnancy. In any case, I was resentful. Here, I thought, was a doctor paternalistically withholding information from someone who had a right to it. Debby, however, took the obstetrician's side. She, not I, was his patient, and in the absence of knowledge about me, he had to call the shot as he saw it.

He would have to do it again four years later, when our second son, Conan, was born. By then fathers in the delivery room were commonplace. Debby asked me if I wanted to be present. She had discussed the matter with the obstetrician, and he agreed that I had a right to be consulted. I thought about it. Though there was every reason to expect the delivery to be normal, another seizure was possible. If something went wrong, how would I know what was happening? Everyone wore a mask. In an emergency there might not be time for a nurse to pull down her mask and tell me what was going on. It was possible that I could unwittingly get in the way and jeopardize the lives of mother and child.

We decided to leave the decision to the doctor. He was the professional and could see the problem from more angles than I. Forthrightly he said he'd rather not have me present. He wanted to minimize the risks. That was all right with me. And in the end, the delivery went smoothly for mother and child—and daddy.

There was, however, one more reproductive medical experience to bear—the single most difficult sequence of events I have experienced in my life. Like most young men, I had considered myself inextinguishable, even charmed. Vaguely, I had thought that having contracted meningitis at age three— the odds against doing so were one in a hundred thousand—would somehow insure me for the rest of my life against further medical catastrophe. In 1980, however, the thunderbolt of chance struck for the second time.

The year before, when Colin was ten and Conan six, Debby and I had decided to limit our family to the two robust sons it had been our good fortune to produce. After thoroughly researching the question, we decided that the best solution was a vasectomy. The procedure was and is simple, is done with a local anesthetic, involves little discomfort, and the risks are tiny—there is only about one failure per thousand vasectomies. So in due course I presented myself one morning for outpatient surgery to a veteran urologist at nearby Evanston Hospital.

Unlike most doctors I had encountered, the urologist was sensitive to my deafness. It was his habit to give vasectomy patients a cut-by-cut, stitch-by-stitch account of the surgery, much like a baseball broadcaster. To ensure that I knew what was going on, he pulled down his gauze mask so that I could read his lips as he gave the play-by-play. That was very decent of him, I thought, but after a few minutes of lying flat on my back while the doctor waved a sharp blade in the most sensitive of my neighborhoods, I decided I would rather not know the details. Until the game was over I looked straight up at the ceiling.

But during the spring of 1980, Debby discovered that she was pregnant, and we were thunderstruck. This was an eventuality we had not anticipated, and in the early days we were shattered. The doctors and nurses at our health maintenance organization seemed cold and disapproving, as if they believed the pregnancy must have been the result of an extramarital affair, and that a quick abortion would be Debby's wish.

The HMO staff's attitude quickly changed after I visited the urologist and the results of the sperm test came in. It was, of course, positive. Somehow the cauterized ends of one of my severed tubes had regenerated themselves enough so that the horses could escape the barn.

Debby and I are both very much in favor of a woman's right to choose between ending a pregnancy and carrying it to term. Together we decided that the best course for us was the latter. We could easily afford a third child; we were uncomfortable with the idea of abortion for simple reasons of convenience. Besides, a couple of boisterous boys bouncing around the house for years made both of us look forward to the prospect of a quiet, civilized daughter. Soon it became an eager anticipation, for an amniocentesis showed that the growing fetus indeed was female as well as healthy.

Meanwhile, I returned to the urologist for a repeat performance. He had also been stunned by the events, and seemed much relieved when we told him that we had decided to treat our seeming misfortune as an unexpected gift. Naturally he would redo the operation without charge. He is one of the most sensitive and compassionate doctors I have ever encountered, and he smiled sadly as he reflected on the irony of having just had to tell one couple that they would never be able to have children, then consulting with another who had proved, the hard way, exactly the opposite. In a few days the deed was again done, and this time he lengthened the odds against another accident by removing a good length of each vas instead of just snipping it.

As summer deepened, so did Debby's pregnancy. Like every other expectant couple, we contentedly ruminated over what to name the baby, what her temperament might be like, how to decorate her room, how her brothers would receive her arrival. With her first tentative kicks she took on a distinct personality in our imaginations. We had never seen her, but she had already become part of our lives.

Then one day a reporter who sat at a desk next to mine tapped me on the shoulder, phone in hand. Her face was white. "Claire Peterson just called," she said. "Meet Debby at the doctor's. Right now."

Instantly, instinctively, I knew what had happened. If Claire, one of our closest friends, had had to call for Debby, something was terribly wrong. Wordlessly—I could not trust my voice not to break—I dashed out of the office and into a taxi. Forty minutes later it drew up at the entrance to the HMO just as Claire and Debby arrived there. Debby began to weep, and so did I.

Earlier in the day she had gone to the hospital for a routine check. There was no

223

heartbeat inside her womb. The baby was dead.

We were devastated, but it was just the beginning of a week-long ordeal. As we took our seats in front of the doctor's desk, he casually placed a box of tissues in front of Debby as if expecting her to crumble into hysterics. "Let's face it," he said briskly. "This pregnancy is over."

But Debby, who has a steely will, had marshaled her emotional resources. She questioned him coolly, with dry eyes and level voice, asking what we had to do next. (He barely acknowledged my presence, as if I were a silent stick of furniture.) She would have to go to the hospital, where labor would be induced, he replied, so that she could deliver the fetus. The procedure, however, couldn't be performed for five days, he said, because the hospital was full.

I will never understand how Debby managed to carry a lifeless child inside her for nearly a week without losing her mind. It's like endlessly carrying your baby's coffin in your arms without being able to lay it down, to relieve your mind and body of an unimaginable burden. But she managed. There was nothing else to be done, and she knew it.

Five days later, just as she prepared to enter the hospital, she was informed that she had to wait still another day. She coldly warned the hospital that if that was necessary, they had better prepare a space for her in the psychiatric ward, because she had come to the end of her rope. They found a bed for her right away. Of all things, it was in the obstetrics ward, right in the middle of scores of mothers and newborns—a place hardly appropriate for the emotional health of a woman who has just lost a child. This was 1980, but it seemed that most doctors and hospitals still wore nineteenth-century horse blinkers so far as their patients' psyches were concerned.

Debby, however, had just begun to plumb her well of resources. She demanded—and got—a bed in another ward. It turned out to be the cancer ward. Fortunately the only bed available there was in a private room, so she did not have to endure the things that go on in such a place. But her real ordeal had not yet begun.

Early in the morning of the sixth day, she was wheeled into a small, windowless room and given drugs to induce labor. The contractions began slowly. I sat at her side, holding her hand and putting cold compresses to her brow at the worst moments. Hours went by, and little happened. Doctors and nurses came and went. They spoke only to her and not to me. Despite her discomfort, she relayed to me what they said. They administered more drugs, which also failed to work. Her pain grew. I sat in a cold sweat, feeling more and more helpless. "What can I do?" I asked a nurse who looked in. She shook her head irritatedly, as if to say, "Nothing." I cursed my deafness for the barrier it had thrown up between me and those in authority. I feared that if I demanded to be told the details of what was happening to my wife, I would be thrown out of the room.

So, as she gritted her teeth against the agony, I held her and soothed her as best I could as the doctor forcibly delivered the fetus. The memory is like a Hieronymus Bosch rendering of the depths of hell, one that I have managed to block from my consciousness for almost a decade. When it was over we were both exhausted and dripping with sweat. She turned to me—the hospital personnel had yet to offer me a single piece of information—and said that she had to go into the operating room for a dilatation and curettage, the scraping of the womb to remove the remaining contents of conception.

At that moment an anesthesiologist entered and said he'd have to inject an anesthetic into the lower spine to allow him to complete the delivery with instruments.

"No!" Debby said, and despite the anesthesiologist's importunings, she would not give in. She had been warned by her neurologist that a caudal anesthetic during or after labor might send her into another seizure and that she should never allow one to be administered. Evidently the anestesiologist wasn't familiar with that peril, or with her medical history. But against her adamant refusal he could not insist.

The procedure, Debby told me, would take about twenty minutes. Meanwhile, I was to wait outside in the fathers' room. An attendant wheeled Debby into the operating room and I sat down alone. Twenty minutes passed. Thirty. No one came. Forty-five. An hour. My stomach turned cold. Had something gone wrong? An hour and fifteen minutes. I stared at the doors to the operating-room area, got up, and peered through the glass. I could see nothing, no one. An hour and a half, and still I saw no one. Except for me, the fathers' room was empty. The clock ticked on. "Has Debby died?" I thought. "Why won't anyone come to tell me?"

After almost two hours had passed, a weary resident came into the room and beckoned. Wordlessly he led me to Debby, lying on a gurney just outside the operating room, nodded, and departed. She was white, drawn and exhausted, but alive. "I'm okay," she said, as tears of relief flooded my cheeks.

Just as Debby had entered the operating theater, a mother delivering twins in the next room had experienced complications, and the obstetrician and his nurses had had to leave Debby alone while they dealt with that time-consuming emergency. Whether no one had thought to inform the deaf man in the fathers' room of the delay, or whether they simply could not spare anyone for the brief moment it would have taken to do so, I don't know.

In the end we both recovered from the ordeal and the mourning, and put them behind us as rapidly as we could. Certainly the humiliation and impotence I felt still stings my memory, but I thank my stars that Debby had the resilience and resourcefulness to compensate for my inability to do the things a hearing husband would have done in the same situation. As in all successful marriages, each spouse's weaknesses are off-set by the strengths of the other.

We chose not to sue. The urologist, we felt, was as much a victim of circumstances as we were; the law of averages had simply caught up with him in the same way as the roulette wheel had once again turned up my number. In no manner did we believe he was negligent. As for the HMO and hospital personnel, their worst sin was that of honest ignorance, the benightedness of the time. Besides, no financial settlement could have compensated us for the pain of our loss. To institute a lawsuit, we thought, would just have been to drag out for years the process of healing.

What caused our baby's death? Possibly a genetic flaw. It might have been exposure to the Coxsackie virus during the early weeks of the pregnancy; both Colin and I had had it at the time. Perhaps the amniocentesis was to blame. We will never know. What is certain is that today the medical profession recognizes the impact of fetal deaths, even those as common as simple miscarriages, on the emotional health of the mother.

Prodded by federal law in some cases, modern medicine also recognizes the right of deaf patients—and of deaf members of patients' families—to instant and complete information in doctors' offices and hospitals. Today every urban hospital worth its Blue Cross contract has at least one lipreading or sign language interpreter on staff. Not only do they make sure that deaf patients understand every word that their doctors tell them: they keep the lines of communication open between deaf patients and the nursing staff. They also address the needs of deaf members of patients' families, sitting with them in the waiting room during surgery—and helping deaf fathers enjoy the miracle of their children's birth in the delivery room.

Like any other father, I took frequent and happy responsibility for feedings and diaperings and baths and other joys of young parenthood. I do feel guilty, just a little and not very often, when I think of how Debby would awaken in the night to a crying baby and quietly slip from our bed, careful not to disturb my sleep. Alone in the kitchen she'd prepare his bottle and clean his bottom while I slept on.

Early in our marriage she had declared that she would stay home and take care of our children when they were young, while I won the daily bread. She was going to be awake at night and weary during the day, she reasoned. It was silly for two people to suffer if only one had to. (That's just one reason why I love her so.) Her decision long antedated the revolution of two-earner families and day-care centers; in those days, mothers almost invariably took on the primary responsibility of child care. Not for Debby, however, a life of soap operas and lunch with the ladies. Three months after Colin was born she began work on a master's degree in library science at Rosary College, and finished it three years later, just a month before Conan came along.

"What is it like being married to a deaf man?" Debby is sometimes asked. "How is it different from marriage to a hearing person?" Her reply: "How should I know? I've been married only once!"

She does say that being unable to talk with me in the dark is probably the worst problem of communication we have. She's tried tracing words on the skin of my back, but all that does is tickle me. Nonetheless, we've developed a rough code for pillow talk. A quick little circular motion of her finger on my arm means "Did you lock the front door before coming up to bed?" Anything more complicated than that requires turning on the bedside light.

And she wishes I would go to the theater with her. She loves the theater, but I miss too much, even sitting in the first row, to truly enjoy a play. She knows how agonizingly antsy sitting for two hours and understanding little can be, so she attends with friends. We do, however, go to the ballet together. Dance is the most visual of the performing arts, and I enjoy it intensely, especially when I can feel the vibrations of the music and match it to the action onstage.

Occasionally I feel that Debby doesn't sympathize enough with my dislike of large parties. In the past she has dragged me to such gatherings despite my having absolutely nothing in common with the people there, simply because she needed an escort and demanded that I do my husbandly duty. On the other hand, she has an exquisite sense of when it is absolutely necessary for me to carry the flag—certain obligatory literary parties are an example—and I cherish that.

In the same way I've sometimes felt that she has regarded my deep latter-day interest in electronic communications devices such as computers and TDDs (successors to the primitive TTYs) as just another expensive hobby. It is not that to me; as I've explained, it's an important way of keeping the walls of isolation from closing in. I have to admit, however, that I've squandered small fortunes on transitory enthusiasms such as photography, tropical aquariums—she still refers to that as "Henry's Fish Period"—and model railroading.

On the other hand, we have so much in common that what we don't or can't share seems exceedingly trivial. We are both writers and readers. We love traveling, especially in the Rocky Mountains. Our value systems are identical; we judge people not by their wealth and possessions but by their intellects and contributions to society. We see eye to eye on family matters, especially the rearing of our boys.

And how has my deafness affected my relations with them? Again, much more is known today than twenty years ago about the psychological consequences hearing children of the deaf often face. Lou Ann Walker's excellent 1986 book *A Loss for Words* told about the awesome responsibilities she faced as a very small child in helping her deaf mother and father deal with the outside world.

Even as a toddler she had to serve as their

ears and voice, dealing with tradesmen, town officials, and lawyers in language she barely understood. She heard hearing people say hurtful, derogatory things about her parents, who spoke in sign language and had very little speech. As a result, she subsumed her identity into theirs; it took many years of adulthood before she was able to function confidently as a hearing person in her own right.

Our pediatrician, who knew something about deaf culture and wrongly assumed that I was a member of it, warned Debby not to force Colin to serve as a go-between for me. "Don't make him handle the telephone for your husband," he said. "It could give him a complex." Possibly it could have, but the doctor was needlessly worried. After all, there was a hearing adult in our household. In practice, Debby and I were home at the same time; a phone call for me usually was from the office, and Colin would simply hand the receiver to her. He knew she knew more than he did about such things. When he grew older and more sophisticated, he would occasionally handle a call. They were so infrequent we never felt that any pressure was being put on him. And, we believe, Conan had the same experience.

As for hearing jeers and catcalls from ignorant oafs: Just once, Debby thinks, did Colin have a bit of trouble with that, when he was about twelve. A fellow seventh-grade Y club member informed Colin that he wasn't going to come to our house for a meeting "because your dumb deaf dad talks funny." Colin, who always has possessed a quick wit and a sharp tongue, immediately retorted, "You're adopted. You don't know who your father is. I know who mine is." And that was that.

Colin, especially, showed an early awareness that his father could not hear. When he was barely a year and a half old, not yet speaking more than a few words, we noticed that he always tried to maneuver into my line of sight when he wanted to talk to me. Before he was two, while riding in the kiddie carrier that sat on the rear of my bicycle, he'd thump me on the back so that I would stop and turn around to see what he had to say.

Almost as soon as both boys were high enough to steal a cookie from the jar on the kitchen counter, they probably had the sense that although their daddy might not be able to hear and that he spoke in a funny way, he still knew how to get along in that great big strange world outside our house. Often I'd take them without their mother to places where they could see how I spoke with unfamiliar people, sometimes having to repeat myself but most often effortlessly. And it cannot have been lost on them that the people their mother and father socialized with were almost all ordinary hearing people, with an occasional deaf guest.

More important, perhaps, life in our family was just like that at their friends' houses: quiet, suburban, mostly unhurried, with occasional patches of frenzied activity when the family packed the car and visited Gramma and Grampa or went camping in Canada or the American Rockies. The boys' childhood, I think, has been just as normal and ordinary as mine was, with their father doing for them exactly what hearing fathers do for their children. Their father has always been there, even to attending their school Christmas musicals, events that are to a deaf man about as exciting as a *Playboy* centerfold is to a blind one. They have had the normal amount of space to grow, and if their father's deafness has been a noticeable part of their surroundings, perhaps it stands out no more than any other stick of family furniture.

Both boys share something special and

unique in their wider worlds: they are expert lipreaders, as good as or even better than their father. That won't surprise anyone in the field of deaf education; study after study has shown that at any age hearing people, being familiar with the rhythms and syntax of spoken language, tend to learn lipreading faster than do the deaf. For Colin and Conan, growing up with lipreading has been much like growing up in a bilingual home. The talent affords both boys a lot of amusement as they silently chat with each other across a crowded, noisy room, sometimes to the disgust of hearing friends who'd like to share in their secrets but can't.

The boys do favor their mother with their inner secrets a bit more than they do their father, just as I did with my own parents. There are probably two reasons. The more important, I think, is the earlier intimacy a child develops with the primary care giver of the ordinary American family unit, the mother. The lesser, subtler reason may be that it has always been easier for Colin and Conan to communicate with their hearing mother than with their deaf father. In the beginning, Debby could understand their first childish speech better than I could. Later, at night, in a darkened room, they could sleepily whisper their last confidences of the day into their mother's ear. If I was there instead of her, I'd have to turn on the light and dazzle their little eyes.

Psychologists ought to be careful about exaggerating this phenomenon, of building it into a nonexistent barrier between hearing child and deaf parent. They must keep in mind that of all the interlocking relationships children develop with their parents, one of the most important is an unspoken one, a kind of companionable silence. Just as my father demonstrated, with wordless example, how to ride a bicycle, how to catch a ball, how to swing a bat, how to wield a paintbrush, how to hammer a nail, and how to saw a board, so have I shown my sons. Some things can be learned only by showing, not by telling, and if we are lucky, our fathers will have a knack for that. Mine did. And as I watch Colin building a wooden cabinet in the basement or Conan rocketing a line drive into left field, I think I did, too.

Finally, there's the matter of their father's position in society. Most deaf breadwinners work at menial jobs if they are unlucky and the blue-collar trades if they are lucky. They may achieve considerable pride and dignity in their work, but early on, children will notice the value society places on their parents' labor. From a very early age, however, Colin and Conan have been aware that their father occupies a position of some respect and consequence in the community. His name is in the paper frequently, his picture in it every weekend. He serves on committees and juries and often travels on business. Can it be lost on the boys that their father perhaps has enjoyed a larger share of good fortune than some others?

————9————

In the beginning Colin couldn't have cared less what his daddy did for a living. When I became book editor of the Chicago *Daily News* in March 1973, he was not yet four. Besides, the week I was appointed his little brother was born, and that was much more important.

The road from the copy desk to the book editorship wasn't without false turns and bumpy passages. I'd dreamed of the job since my days as a part-time critic in Wilmington, but such a goal had seemed almost unattainable. I had had little experience as a critic, and assumed that heavy-duty academic credentials were also necessary. All that was needed, it turned out, was a love of books and a willingness to pay a few dirty-fingernailed dues.

In 1970 one of my night desk mentors was elevated to the job of assistant managing editor in charge of features. He suggested I move with him to his new department to get a taste of another kind of journalism. The proposal at first seemed unattractive. Why give up local, national, and foreign news—matters of consequence—for the fluff of society columns, food and fashion stories, and comic strips? That was *women's* stuff. Features was where the lady writers hung out, while we hardened cigar chompers held sway in the city room, except for two "girl reporters" who covered "safe" beats such as the library and school boards. (One was Lois Wille, who later would win two Pulitzer Prizes, and the other was Georgie Anne Geyer, later the star of the *Daily News's* foreign service and a renowned globe-trotting syndicated columnist.)

But a new wind was beginning to sweep through American daily journalism. We didn't know it at the time, but events—prodded by the rise of feminism and the Vietnam War—had started to blur the line between journalism aimed at men and that intended for women, as well as the roles of those who did the writing and reporting. A new sense of social responsibility was beginning to seep into the features columns. Coverage of high-society charity balls came to seem less important than stories about birth control and Montessori schools. Service

241

journalism—food and fashion—was still timely, especially in attracting advertising, but was no longer the queen of the features department.

Working the features copy desk gave me experience in handling these broader kinds of stories, which we called, a bit contemptuously in the beginning, "soft" stories. "Hard" stories concerned murders, stock-market swings, and the latest body count in the Ia Drang Valley. I soon noticed that features writers seemed to take a different approach to their subjects. They tended to be more thoughtful, less dependent on formula, and not quite so driven by sensation as their hard-bitten confreres on "cityside." I began to learn new respect for them.

All this is not to say that copyreading in the features department was an unalloyed adventure. There was also a great deal of routine drudgery that involved checking recipes, clipping canned sewing-column features, and dealing with reader-participation contests, and I hated and was bored by it.

But along with the enervating dog work came other opportunities. Sharing the features department with the "women's pages" was the arts and amusements department, which covered movies, theater, nightlife, art, classical and popular music—and books. The *Daily News's* book section was part of *Panorama*, one of the country's first and best weekend arts and entertainment supplements.

At its head was Richard Christiansen, who also doubled as second-string theater critic behind the distinguished syndicated columnist Sydney J. Harris. Dick (who is now the entertainment editor and theater critic of the Chicago *Tribune*) is not only a first-rate and demanding "pencil editor" but also every bit as good a writer as any of his critics. A smile of approval from him was and is as rare and bright as a shiny new gold coin. I didn't think I could meet his exacting standards.

But Van Allen Bradley, the paper's veteran literary editor and a renowned rare-book specialist, presided over the book columns. Like so many older editors of those times, he loved to take young journalists under his wing and help them along in their careers. He had the time and space to do so, for those were still relaxed days in newspapering, when staffs were much larger and less pressured than they are today.

As soon as I told him that I had written book reviews in Wilmington a few years earlier, he turned to his commodious cabinet of review copies and pulled down a clutch of first novels. Why not try an omnibus review of these? he asked. He liked the result, published it, and paid me the munificent sum of $20, the standard reviewer's fee of the time.

Van introduced me to the works of Malcolm Cowley and Edmund Wilson, who were not lofty academic theorists but journalists, working critics who rolled up their sleeves and took a reader's-eye view of newly published books. Not for them the arcane mysteries of textual criticism in the classics but the simple questions: "Is this book worth reading? Why or why not?" Aimed at the intelligent, educated, but nonspecialist newspaper and magazine reader, their criticism was broad, even rough-and-ready, yet rooted in careful scholarship and delivered in graceful prose.

Wilson especially found pearls in places other critics would dismiss as trivial. He thought, for example, that the Sherlock Holmes stores were "literature on a humble not ignoble level. . . . The old stories are literature, not because of the conjuring tricks and the puzzles, not because of the lively melodrama . . . but by virtue of imagination and style."

These were eye-opening words to a reader who had approached literature chiefly as an exercise in scholarly inquiry, and they made me read Conan Doyle in a new way, as well as Dickens and other authors once considered purveyors of popular trash. Literature, Wilson taught me, belonged to the people, not the professors. He showed how even lowly entertainments could be written with as much skill and insight as works of high culture, and some of them would last.

I soon began to contribute reviews regularly, and after a time also began to write *Panorama*'s weekly column on paperbacks. By this time I had been "promoted" laterally to production editor for *Panorama*. The job entailed handling not only all the copy and headlines for the section but also page layout and especially composing-room work, directing printers in the makeup of the pages. But now, for the first time in my newspaper career, my deafness seemed to be a dragging anchor. The composing rooms of the old days were noisy places, filled with the clatter of Linotypes, the rattle of heavy-wheeled page trucks, the hammering of machinists, the whine of conveyor belts whisking copy down from the editors on the floor above, and the shouts of "straw bosses," or sub-foremen. I did not have an easy time making myself understood over the din.

At least in the beginning, the printers resented me, and some of their resentment was justified. I had had the misfortune to learn the basics of composing-room tasks from an impatient, high-strung editor who believed the only way to deal with printers was as an adversary who watched their every move critically. Not for a while did I discover that printers, perhaps the most intelligent and thoughtful workers in the skilled trades, responded best to treatment as equals. They had a stubborn pride and would not be pushed.

Not a few, I am convinced, also distrusted me because I was deaf, and for complex reasons. For a long time, the printing trade was a haven for deaf workers, because many of its skills don't require the ability to communicate easily. On a major metropolitan newspaper such as the *Daily News*, however, the deaf were limited largely to Linotype keyboarding and proofreading, both solitary pursuits. Foremen passed them the few orders they needed with paper and pencil or in crude sign language. The deaf didn't work the elite jobs "on the line" as page makeup specialists. And though a skilled worker's production was respected by his hearing union mates, his inability to communicate easily with them—and sometimes the cultural eccentricities of his deafness—ensured his second-class status. To some of the hearing printers, I was a "dummy" who was trying to rise above his station, and therefore was not to be taken seriously. Many didn't want to follow my requests. (Not orders; no editor who wants to get his product out on deadline ever gives orders to a printer.)

Also, the early 1970s were a time when everyone knew that cast-metal "hot type" was on the way out, soon to be replaced by phototypesetting and pasted-up page makeup. That new technology would eliminate more than 75 percent of the jobs in the composing room. A few printers regarded my intrusive presence as a deaf editor as part of the wave of the future.

I also received no sympathy from the deaf printers themselves. Why should they have given me any? Not being able to hear didn't make me one of them—not unless I used sign language. I couldn't communicate with them any better than could a "hearie" straw boss. I felt awkward among them and they with me.

For many months I truly felt like an outsider in the *Daily News*'s composing room. The very depths came one Friday afternoon during my first year in the *Panorama* job. I was having a sweaty, frustrating time trying to communicate with a lone printer, a substitute for the vacationing regular makeup man. There was much to be done on the *Panorama* pages, just ninety minutes away from final "lockup," and we were falling further and further behind. I tried to shout above the din of printers a few feet away, hammering together the last pages of the final-markets edition of the Friday paper before its own deadline. The printer, doubly frustrated by the unfamiliar job and the peculiar babble of the editor trying to direct him, turned and threw up his hands before his compatriots. "This *dummy!*" he shouted.

I saw his words and boiled with rage. The printer was a black man, and I am ashamed to say that I came close to replying in kind, with a racial epithet. But somehow I bit the word down and just glared silently at the fellow, who dropped his eyes in embarrassment as he realized that I had understood him. "I know what you said," I thought fiercely, hoping he could read my mind as my face grew redder and redder. "And I'm not going to forget."

We both, however, forgave. Tempers often flared under deadline pressure in the composing room, but real grudges were rare. After that, whenever we passed each other on the composing-room floor, that printer and I would nod silently to each other, sometimes with a slight smile. I don't know what went through his mind. Perhaps he was acknowledging that I was the aggrieved party in that little dustup and that it was good of me not to take the issue any further.

After the first year, however, the printers and I settled in more comfortably with each other, although some of the old-timers did keep their distance. I became good friends with a few of them, and one even invited me home to the biggest, most elaborate Italian dinner his wife could produce. Winning eventual acceptance by this tough, proud bunch gave me a good deal of satisfaction.

Nonetheless, under the best of circumstances the *Panorama* job was a difficult, sweaty one, because the composing-room work was squeezed in largely at slack times between the daily paper's six or more editions. We never locked up more than five minutes before deadline, and many was the time we blew it by ten or fifteen minutes, inviting frenzied phone calls from the pressroom, which had its own deadline. On a few occasions we missed the late commuter trains carrying the early state editions of the weekend paper to the far corners of Illinois, and stern inquiries came down from the front office.

When the book editorship fell open in early 1973, I immediately applied. Dick Christiansen had left the *Daily News* to take over the helm of a fledgling city magazine, and the book editor, M. W. Newman, moved into his position. Van Allen Bradley had retired just two years before.

The book editorship of a major metropolitan newspaper is a post of some prestige, and it normally goes to a writer or editor of some renown, often a published author. Though I'd had regular weekly bylines as a reviewer and as the contributor of the little column on paperbacks, and had built up a small reputation on the paper as a competent stylist, I was still a nobody. But I held a few good cards.

For one thing, there was only one other applicant from within the paper, a reporter who'd written an excellent literary biography. He was well respected and a better writer than I. But he was also a prickly, difficult fellow, and nobody on *Panorama* needed another burr under the saddle. Moreover, the paper was not inclined to go outside to hire a distinguished and expensive name. By then the slow leaks in circulation, the paper's lifeblood, had turned into a raging hemorrhage. Marshall Field, the owner of the paper, had long before ordered budgetary belt tightening, including a clampdown on salaries.

I was available, and I was cheap. The paper could pay me the minimum Newspaper Guild critic's scale. Nobody knew if I could truly do the job, but I hadn't bungled the ones I had had, and in some of them I'd even acquitted myself creditably. To some of my superiors I seemed a good risk. Perhaps in the post I could build a wider reputation. Again, as had happened so often in my life, people saw enough potential in me to persuade themselves to take a chance.

In the beginning of my new job, I felt pinched by my inability to use the telephone. Much of the book editor's life deals with selecting books for review from the hundreds of galley proofs and finished copies that arrive from publishers each week. Once those books are selected, reviewers must be found for them. Fortunately, Van Allen Bradley had built up a thick card file of reviewers, many of them distinguished authors, and his successors had added to it. Picking prospective reviewers for a given book wasn't a difficult task. Getting hold of them was.

Couldn't I ask a secretary or an editorial assistant to call them? Why, certainly, the managing editor said, whenever they're not busy. He was certain they'd be happy to help me out. The features department, however, had a normal complement of secretaries and editorial assistants, which is to say very few—three worn and harassed women to do gofer chores for the whole department of more than fifty reporters and editors. That was all the impoverished *Daily News* could afford. There are no luxuries at a newspaper on its last legs.

They tried, bless them, they tried. But it just didn't work. All they had time to say to the prospective reviewers was something rushed and breathless, like "I'm-calling-for-Henry-Kisor-book-editor-of-the-*Daily-News*-and-would-you-review-the-new-book-by-so-and-so?"

An abrupt solicitation like that would not

do when all the book editor could offer the reviewer was $25 ($50 if he happened to be a famous writer) and the competition paid three, four, or even five times that. No. One had to approach the matter with care and indirection, greasing the way with a little flattery, and persuade the prospective reviewer to appreciate that public understanding of the book at hand would be ill served in the absence of the reviewer's considered and invaluable opinion.

And if the prospective reviewer asked point-blank if the chances of *his* next volume earning a notice in the *Daily News* would be improved by his consenting to take the proffered book, one had to find new ways of saying no without quite appearing to do so. Promises like that couldn't be kept in book sections so small that barely a dozen volumes could be reviewed each week.

So it fell to the U.S. Postal Service to carry my pleas. As in Wilmington, I felt like a suitor wooing from afar. Three-sentence notes wouldn't do, either. In the beginning, when I was still new, I'd compose long letters introducing myself as inheritor of the distinguished legacy of the previous book editors, then allowing as how they had spoken so highly of the recipient of the letter, and it was with high hopes on behalf of the eager readers of the Chicago *Daily News* that I proposed he review the latest book by so-and-so. Much of it must have been nauseating and all of it transparent. Enough of it, however, was sufficiently amusing so that perhaps 25 percent of the prospects said yes.

When they said no, I had to scramble to find another prospect in time to get the book to him and the review back, to get into print just as finished copies of the volume arrived in the stores. After all, there were two other competing book sections in town, at the *Sun-Times* and the *Tribune,* and this was the city celebrated in Ben Hecht and Charles MacArthur's play *The Front Page,* in which reporters commit all but mayhem to get the story before the competition. Even book editors hate to get beaten.

When time was truly pressing, I'd ask the editorial assistants to make those quick phone calls and hope for the best. Often I'd take the calls home to Debby and explain the situation to her so that she could make them. She never complained but used her best honeyed tones to sweet-talk the reviewers into doing my bidding, and more often than not was successful. However, I always hated to ask her to make these calls. Relying on other people to do my work has always frayed my ego, and it still does. Taking my work home for my wife to do was especially troubling. Deaf people, by and large, dislike being what they consider bothersome to others and will walk an extra ten miles to avoid it. But for me there was no other choice if the job was to be done.

In practical terms, all this fuss about soliciting reviews meant less time for me to do the other tasks of a book editor: writing weekly reviews and occasional long profiles of authors. To make matters worse, I am a slow writer at the best of times. In the 1970s, when we still used typewriters, it would take all day for me to turn out a simple 800-word book review on the enormous old Underwood upright I inherited from my predecessor, Bill Newman.

Bill, who has written Pulitzer Prize-worthy prose as an urban affairs specialist for more than half a century, shares with his brother Edwin, the television commentator, the family's saturnine eyebrows and love of heroic puns. For a review I did of a volume about the painful personal life of the *New Yorker* humorist James Thurber, Bill wrote this headline: "Great Jokes from Little Achings Grow."

Bill taught me one of the most valuable lessons a journalist can ever learn: a good writer gets right to the point, says his say, then puts the pencil down and leaves. Newspaper readers have neither the time nor the inclination for self-conscious literary confection. When he edited my first author profile, he held the copy between two fingers and announced with disdain, "This story needs to be shaken by the scruff of its neck." He killed its first ten paragraphs, most of which lyrically described the sundappled autumn leaves on the lawn of Jack Conroy, the great old proletarian novelist of the 1930s, in Moberly, Missouri. Then, with a deftly written opening sentence, Bill sat me down in Conroy's living room, the first question on my lips. The piece was much praised and even has been anthologized, but the prose was mostly Newman's. And like all great editors, he let me take the credit for it.

Unlike Bill, I am not a savant who can compose an entire piece in his mind, then sit down and unburden himself cleanly and clearly on a few sheets of paper, without a single typographical error or wasted word. I have trouble assembling thoughts on the blackboard of my brain. I must commit them to paper before I can perceive how they are related to one another. I sometimes wonder whether this inability to manipulate abstractions wholly in the mind is directly related to my deafness, to how I learned to use language all those years ago with Doris Mirrielees' methods. Perhaps pushing cardboard strips of sentences and words around the table with her "Chart Work" technique became so deeply ingrained in my psyche that to this day I need the help of visual supports in order to arrange my thoughts.

That may just be a silly rationalization, for many distinguished hearing authors have complained that they can't think without paper and pencil, either. The English novelist E. M. Forster, for instance, always refused face-to-face interviews with the press, because he worried about his ability to answer questions clearly and coherently. He would do so only in writing, so that he could work out his ideas on paper. "How do I know what I think," he argued, "unless I can see what I say?"

And so my working technique was to create a paragraph, rip the sheet from the typewriter, and fuss over it with a pencil, tucking bedraggled sentences under the covers and smoothing the pillows until everything looked fresh and rested. Then I'd roll a new sheet of paper into the typewriter and retype the paragraph. Invariably there was another word to be changed, another phrase to be recast—on a clean new page, of course. Only when the paragraph was perfect could I go on to the next one, and if more than two paragraphs occupied a page, I'd have to re-type the whole thing to get the second one right. At the end of the day I'd be afloat in a sea of wadded-up paper; it must have taken the better part of a ream of copy paper for me to produce a single five-page, double-spaced book review.

Call it obsessive-compulsive neatness or a yen for perfection, this phenomenon is hardly rare among writers, and I am certain that a psychologist who plowed through the stuffed wastebaskets of my psyche would find the cause in a childhood event as simple and mundane as my toilet training. And when others display this quirk, I respect it. I cherish writers who take the time and ex-pense to make a long-distance phone call to change a single word in their reviews for the sake of precision. They *care,* and that's all too rare in a profession such as newspaper-ing, in which "good enough" has begun to edge out "as best as one can" as a criterion of craftsmanship.

One of the watersheds of my life occurred when the *Daily News* (and its sister paper, the morning *Sun-Times*) converted to computerized phototypesetting in 1977. Overnight our typewriters disappeared, replaced by video display terminals wired to an enormous mainframe computer deep in the bowels of the building. There was some grumbling among reporters and editors over being dragged into the Computer Age, but soon "bleeders" like me realized that the coming of the VDT enabled us to toss off the bloody shackles of struggling over every paragraph. On a video monitor we could make changes instantaneously, pulling, twisting, and tying the loose ends of our prose into neat knots, making minute changes quickly and easily without having to retype entire pages. What had taken me eight hours to create now required ninety minutes—less if I was under deadline pressure.

The VDT allowed me for the first time to function as a genuine literary critic as well as a book review editor, reading a book and producing a column on it every weekend as well as assembling a book section. Writing author profiles, another important part of the book editor's job, also became easier. A

3,000-word profile of a novelist no longer took all week to write; the VDT cut the time to a day or two.

What wasn't helped was the long task of woodshedding the profile, doing the homework before interviewing an author. That job still takes me longer than it does others, and this is directly related to my deafness. When I do an interview, the chances are that I will be meeting the writer for the first time. How easy will the author be to lipread? Given the nature of literature, we will be talking about highly abstract topics, in words not often used with ordinary speech. How will I be able to understand what my subject is saying? As I've said, much of the success of lipreading lies in being able to anticipate the words and thoughts others will employ. The more familiar I am with the person to whom I am talking, the more accurate my context-guessing will be. The only way to achieve this familiarity is to spend many hours doing research, skimming the author's previous books, if not reading them in their entirety, as well as digging up and studying every interview of the author one can find and every public pronouncement he might have made. It's like building up a thick dossier on a spy.

But no matter how many hours I spend trying to get inside an author's skin, to find out how he thinks and talks, they won't be enough. I may understand most of what the author says during the interview, but I also may—no, *will*—miss some vital statements, and forget others. Because I must keep my eyes on my subject's face, I cannot take notes. If I look down just for an instant at what I'm writing, I'll lose track of the conversation. Hence I must rely on a tape recorder and the transcript typed from it not only to refresh my memory but also to tell me the things the author said that I didn't understand during the interview.

During my first few years in the book editor's job, getting a tape transcribed was a chore. The overworked secretaries at the *Daily News* had no extra time to help me out. Hence I asked Debby if she'd type up the tapes, and in the beginning was able to get the paper to pay her a meager $25 or so for each transcript. Later the assistant managing editor in charge of parsimony told me that the budgetary turnip had been squeezed so tight that no blood was left to pay even that.

Asking Debby to do this work gratis was unfair to her. But she knew, bless her, that these interviews were important to my career, and insisted on making time to do the job. My speech is harder to understand on tape than it is in person, and many transcribers, especially hired temporary secretaries unaccustomed to my speech, cannot follow what I say. The transcriptions often will be utterly one-sided—all answers, no questions. In practice that's not much of a problem. If I can't remember what I said, there's my notebook of prepared questions as a reminder.

But Debby, intimately accustomed to every vagary in my speech, was able to render verbatim everything I said. And being a bookish person herself (she not only is a professional librarian but also has written a monthly column on children's books for years), she knows the sometimes technical language of literary talk. What's more, she always made certain to indicate the tone of the interviewee's voice as well as the background noises, such as chuckles and moans, that colored his words. Unless instructed otherwise, most transcribers will simply type up flatly what is said, not how it is said. Unless I am alert, I might present an author's intended irony as a bald statement exactly the opposite of what he meant.

Sometimes she'd even go on the interviews with me if they were local. I'd make sure to hold them in the best restaurants in Chicago (the author's publisher footed the bill, of course!) so that she'd at least get a good meal for her pains. We didn't need to tape these encounters; she took copious notes instead, and that saved considerable time.

This state of affairs continued until the awful day in 1978 when Marshall Field finally threw in the towel and announced the closing of the historic old *Daily News*. I left for home expecting that I'd be out of a job in a couple of weeks, but almost before I got out of the building a reporter called me back. Our managing editor wanted to talk to me.

The staffs of the *Daily News* and Field's morning paper, the *Sun-Times*, were being consolidated. The managing editor was moving into the same job at the *Sun-Times*, he said, and he wanted to take me along as book editor. The morning daily's book editorship had been vacant for years, the tasks handled by the paper's arts and amusements editor, but Field wanted a full complement of staff to compete with the *Tribune*, now the only other paper in town.

On the spot I said yes. The choice was obvious. There are perhaps fewer than twenty full-time book editorships on American newspapers, and such jobs are hard to get. Besides, the *Sun-Times* was a profitable paper, and it could afford to assign a competent editorial assistant to make my phone calls as part of her regular tasks.

I couldn't have been luckier. Shirlee De Santi, a veteran of the newspaper wars under half a dozen or more book and arts editors, seemingly knew—and knows—everybody in the publishing business. She also has a soft and gentle telephone manner that could charm the wallpaper off a ballroom. More than one author has told me he really didn't want to review a book but just couldn't refuse Shirlee.

The paper also saw to it that after an author interview a competent staff stenographer would provide me with a full transcript of an interview at the office the very next day. And they have; I have nothing to complain about. But few stenographers have displayed the painstaking skill and insight with which Debby converted those tapes to transcripts.

All that fuss over researching and transcribing an interview may sound like a lot of trouble just to produce a few thousand words of copy that's going to end up the next day at the bottom of a reader's kitty-litter box. It *is* time-consuming. But in at least one way it often gives me a certain advantage over less prepared journalists.

Very early in our interviews, my subjects will suddenly realize that I take them, and their work, seriously enough to have spent a great deal of time preparing for the occasion. All too often they have had to deal with vapid media creatures whose first question is "Tell me, what's your book about?" and who then parrot a list of questions the publisher's publicity people have provided in a press kit accompanying the volume. Some of these authors are almost embarrassingly grateful that an interviewer actually would take the time to read their latest work, and they are more than forthcoming with their answers to my questions.

Years ago, for instance, I talked with William Styron just before his novel *Sophie's Choice* arrived in the bookstores. When he ushered me into the living room of his Connecticut home, he seemed chilly and suspicious, as if a deaf writer interviewing an author was an outlandish *People* magazine notion, like photographing him in his bathtub. By then I had hit upon the gambit of devoting my very first question to some obscure point in the book, to demonstrate to the author right at the beginning that I'd done my homework. I don't recall what the question was, but it had to do with his intention in creating a minor character who made a brief appearance in a single chapter.

Styron slapped his leg in delight and a broad smile appeared on his face. He hunkered forward and gave me two hours instead of the customary sixty minutes, and it was one of the best interviews I have ever had. If he had any suspicions or reservations about my deafness from that point on, he never showed them.

Just once did my deafness call into question the success of an interview, but the result was happy. I asked Bernard Malamud, who was preparing to publish his novel *Dubin's Lives*, if he would mind if I taped an interview with him. He wrote back to say that he indeed would mind. Some novelists, especially those with one eye on posterity, have less faith in the spoken word than the written one and worry about the existence of tapes containing imprecise oral statements that might compete with their carefully considered prose. They prefer their obiter dicta to be their own, not filtered through the prose of journalists. Malamud was such a novelist.

But when I explained the situation and proposed that I destroy the tape and the transcript after the interview appeared in print, Malamud agreed. Perhaps because our negotiations had made him wonder just how successful this enterprise was going to be, he seemed quiet and reserved for the first half hour of our interview, but eventually the chill burned off and we had a true conversation, not just a simple question-and-answer session, the kind that makes a literary profile exceptional. That was because he turned out to be easy to lipread.

If the authors are difficult for me to understand—and fortunately, there aren't many of them—our talks don't take on a conversational life. More than once an interview has ended without my understanding a single word the interviewee said. The transcript reveals controversial statements not questioned, promising avenues not taken. Generally, however, there's enough material for a publishable piece, and most writers, when asked, will give me their phone numbers in case I need to call them to fill in the gaps.

Edward Abbey was such a writer. When

the late author of *The Monkey Wrench Gang* and *Desert Solitaire* sat across a table from me one morning in a Tucson hotel, I could not for the life of me understand one word he said. He spoke with considerable expression but deep from the back of his throat, with very little lip movement. I think he knew I was working in the dark, and he made up for it by playing to the tape recorder, rattling off amusing and outrageous answers to my questions as well as thoughtful and considered replies. Sure, he said after the interview, I could call him later if needed. It wasn't necessary. Fortunately I'd asked the right questions and he'd given back highly quotable answers.

This sort of solicitude is not necessarily indicative of a caring character who wants to help out a handicapped journalist. Writers who appreciate the value of publicity know that eager cooperation helps sell their books, and they'll work hard to make the interview a success. On the other hand, a lack of concern can be revealing.

One such interview was with Anthony Burgess, the British novelist. He was in Chicago on a publicity tour for a new novel, and we met along with Debby and his publisher's publicist in a downtown restaurant. He spent much of the interview gazing boredly out the window, offering desultory answers to my questions. A couple of times the publicist had to elbow him sharply to pay attention to me. I don't know whether he couldn't handle my deafness, as some people cannot, or he was simply tired and bored with the long, a-new-city-a-day publicity tour American publishers require of their authors. Whatever the truth, the result was one of the shortest and least inspiring pieces I've ever done on a major writer.

Burgess's countryman Eric Ambler, the spy novelist, turned out to be a wholly different sort of Englishman. He, too, was doing a long, grueling tour (one he would discuss with considerable distaste in his memoirs) for a new espionage tale. I met him with a photographer in his hotel room and immediately got off to a bad start. Instead of lurking in the background, the photographer, an aggressive young man with a street-punk demeanor, climbed all over Ambler, who was trying to listen carefully to the first question from his interviewer, who had a peculiar way of speaking. Suddenly the photographer rapped Ambler sharply in the leg with a lighting tripod. "See here!" the Englishman said severely. "I won't have this!

You wait outside and come back after we're done talking!"

"We've blown it," I thought. But Ambler, ever the professional, had agreed to do a publicity tour, and by God he was going to make it a success no matter how difficult his interlocutors. He sat back down and in forty-five minutes gave me one of the liveliest, most readable interviews I've ever had. And a year or so later the punky young photographer, Anthony Suau, moved on to the Denver *Post*, where he redeemed himself with a Pulitzer Prize.

In small ways my deafness sometimes reveals interesting bits of character about the authors I encounter. Early on, I tried taping luncheon interviews, only to discover that the background noise, of which I was unaware, often nearly obliterated everything that was said. One talk I had with the illustrator Maurice Sendak in a Manhattan restaurant was very nearly ruined by the waiters' clattering of cutlery and china on nearby tables, and only Debby's careful listening as she constantly wound and rewound the tape saved the piece.

But when my interview subjects are journalists or former journalists, they often anticipate such problems. Tom Wolfe insisted that we talk about his book *The Right Stuff* at lunch, and when I hesitated said, "Trust me." We ate at his favorite Italian restaurant in New York City, an establishment jutting out on the sidewalk that featured tiny private cubicles just large enough for a table for four, with a door that could be shut to seal out waiterly noises. The meal was excellent, the interview splendid, and the tape crystal clear.

When I spoke with Susan Cheever, daughter of the great novelist John Cheever and a competent storyteller in her own right, the locale was the Houghton Mifflin offices in New York City just across from Grand Central Terminal.

"Henry, let's move to another room," she said before I could ask my first question. On the street a couple of stories below, two powerful jackhammers were singing a duet—not quite loudly enough for me to feel the vibrations, but with enough vigor to blanket a conversation on tape. Susan, a former *Newsweek* reporter, had sized up the situation quickly—and averted what might have been a disaster.

Only rarely have I mentioned my deafness in the profiles I write—it is usually irrelevant, and for a long time I resisted the idea, not wishing to put my handicap on display —but this particular little incident clearly was worth using in the piece, for it illustrated its subject's caring and observant nature.

In the same way, Edward Hoagland displayed a quick resourcefulness worth noting in the article I wrote about him. The essayist and novelist has a stutter that sometimes can be paralytic. Getting his first word out often takes a few moments, and at our meeting in his Greenwich Village apartment I think his concern over making himself clearly understood to me caused him to freeze more than usual. Repeatedly he leaned toward me, reddening with the effort, saying, "D-d-d-d-d-d," unable to get out the rest of the word.

Hoagland, who has written eloquently, if ruefully, about the devilment his affliction can cause, is not the kind who lets frustration defeat him. He stood up, crooked his finger, and led me into his study. Motioning me to stand behind his desk as he sat down, he fed a sheet of paper into his typewriter and tapped out: "Let's do it this way. It'll save time and grief."

And so, for an hour, we conversed in that manner, I speaking and Hoagland typing, and the piece turned out to be full of lively, crisp, fascinating quotes. It was the only out-of-town interview I've ever conducted without needing a tape recorder—and the only one in which the interviewee provided his own instant transcript.

Another such episode occurred with the novelist Joseph Heller. He's one of my favorite interview subjects, because he is not only easy to lipread but also one of the most voluble and thoughtful people I have ever encountered. He answers one-sentence questions with well-considered oral essays hundreds of words long, covering all possible avenues of digression. The worst difficulty in writing the interview is deciding what to throw out in order to keep the piece to a manageable length.

When I talked with Heller about his novel *God Knows* in 1984, he was just recovering from a long bout with Guillain-Barré syndrome, a mysterious condition that temporarily paralyzes every muscle in the body. Right away I noticed that he was not as easy for me to understand as in our three or four previous meetings, because his upper lip was still paralyzed. A bit more than a year later, just before he and his friend Speed Vogel published their joint book on Heller's hospitalization and recovery, I visited the novelist at his Long Island home. That stiff upper lip gave me an opener I'll wager no other journalist had:

EAST HAMPTON, N.Y.—The last time I had talked with Joseph Heller, it was the summer of 1984. His upper lip was still partly paralyzed by the mysterious malady that had felled him in late 1981. He had trouble forming "m" sounds, making it hard for me, a deaf lip-reader, to understand him.

But a year later, riding in his car from the railroad station to his home in this Long Island resort town, I could detect in his speech no remnant of Guillain Barré syndrome. His step was firm, his gestures controlled, his driving relaxed.

My deafness, of course, gave me an entree to the presence of Walker Percy. Just before his novel *The Second Coming* was published in 1980, I wrote to him asking for an interview. He wasn't going to be at home in Louisiana, he replied, but in Toronto for a conference on semiotics, the study of signs and symbols, which is his avocation. Ordinarily he wouldn't have given an interview there, but he wanted to see what another product of Doris Mirrielees was like.

It was then that I first heard the dramatic story of the Percys' discovery of their daughter's deafness. Ann was just eleven months old when Percy and his wife, Mary Bernice ("Bunt"), took her out into the fields near their home one day. Someone had reported a rattlesnake on the property, and Percy took along a shotgun. They found the reptile and he dispatched it. When Ann, cradled in Bunt's arms, did not react to the blast of the shotgun, the Percys realized that something was amiss with her hearing. A short time later they met Miss Mirrielees.

For our second interview, in 1987 for Percy's *The Thanatos Syndrome*, Debby insisted on flying to Louisiana with me. She wanted to meet the Percys, and, like them, she wanted to see what would happen when two of Miss Mirrielees' pupils met for the first time. Would two deaf people who read lips be able to communicate easily with each other? It turned out that to each other Ann and I were just like hearing neighbors, and our meeting provided some offbeat personal interest to what might have been a routine literary article.

On one occasion deafness provided an underlying theme for an entire interview, one that gave me a great deal of insight into myself as well as the author. The piece follows in its entirety:

NEW YORK—It is not often that a deaf person learns something from a blind one. But I did from Ved Mehta, a celebrated writer for *The New Yorker*.

His fifth volume of autobiography—*Sound-Shadows of the New World*—is to be published next month. It is the fascinating story of Mehta's adolescence at the Arkansas School for the Blind in Little Rock after arriving from his native India at age 15 in 1949.

As are all his other memoirs, this one is much more than the history of a person who happens to be physically handicapped. It is also about what it was like for a youngster from another culture to grow up in the United States in a certain time and place, and it resonates with universal experience and shared emotion.

Best of all, it is written in prose as clear and musical as a mountain brook, with a wealth of candid detail only a prodigious memory could provide.

Some particulars of *Sound-Shadows* spoke to me in a way they may not to other readers: they made me relive many special events of my childhood and youth, for Mehta and I have a good deal in common. We share a profession. And meningitis robbed him of his sight at age 4; the same disease took my hearing at age 3.

We both learned to make our other senses compensate for the loss. Early on I developed an acute sensitivity to vibrations and the movement of air. A creak of floorboards and a puff of wind from an opened door often will announce that someone has entered the room behind me.

Likewise, Mehta sharpened his "facial vision," a kind of blind person's radar. Its precise nature is elusive, but it helps those lucky enough to have it to detect the presence of obstacles without needing artificial aids, such as canes and seeing-eye dogs.

Most important, however, we both learned to be independent. As a young student at an impecunious state school, Mehta may not have received much of an academic education—that would come later, at Pomona College, Oxford and

Harvard—but he shunned canes and did everything he could to get rid of "blind-isms," physical idiosyncrasies that signaled sightlessness.

So, also, did I avoid "deafisms" such as sign language. Whether it was by chance or my parents' design, I grew up entirely among hearing people, speaking and lipreading well enough, however imperfectly, to consider myself a normal person. Sign language was for those unlucky enough to be born deaf or lose their hearing before they had developed speech. Those who needed sign, I thought, were condemned to a narrow, limited world, and I felt sorry for them.

When I met Mehta early one morning in New York, I half-expected an intense fellow, perhaps one constantly on edge, always out to prove himself. But the slim 51-year-old man who greeted me gravely in his living room was relaxed and dignified, with a gentle smile. He gave a fatherly peck and a pat to his 14-month-old daughter, Sage, before sending her off with his wife of three years, Linn.

He hesitated before passing through the doorway to the library where we would talk, as if he knew he was off center, then adjusted his step to enter straight through the middle. "Were you using facial vision for that?" I asked. "What is facial vision, anyway?"

"Sometimes my mind isn't on what I'm doing," he said with a chuckle. "I tend to be a dreamy person, like most writers. If I'm not concentrating, it's quite likely that I'd go off center. Also, you got me in the morning before I had my first cup of coffee.

"As for facial vision, it's not clear that scientists know what it is. There's much misunderstanding about it. I go by sound, echoes, the air pressure around the ears. When I'm in a familiar place, I know where the door is and, as I poetically call it, 'where the sound-shadows change.' That's an open, more airy place."

"Can you always depend on facial vision?" I asked, thinking about how my knack for lipreading can desert me at the worst possible moments. The compensations handicapped people can make are remarkable, but they're by no means foolproof.

"It lets me down when there's a pneumatic drill or terrific wind, or at the airport with a lot of planes," he said. "If there are a lot of blanketing sounds, then my facial vision suffers. A jackhammer almost completely paralyzes me; I can't tell where I am or what I'm doing."

Ironically, another situation in which Mehta's facial vision falters is in "an absolutely open field without trees. For facial vision to be most effective, there has to be an object to which I can establish some kind of relationship—and also there has to be a fair degree of quiet so that I can discriminate between different kinds kids of sound-shadows."

Facial vision serves Mehta well enough so that he can stand at a busy Manhattan intersection, listening for changes in the thrum of traffic and for the click of crossing signals, and make his way across the street as agilely as any other New Yorker—and without a cane or a guide dog. Facial vision does not, however, guard him from such hazards as two-foot-long standpipes jutting at waist level from the side of a building.

"Do you think a seeing-eye dog could be of some help?" I asked.

"Not to me," he replied. "As with people who have all their faculties, the abilities of the blind and perhaps the deaf vary a lot. Certain blind people, especially those who lose their eyesight late in life, find a seeing-eye dog very useful. But when I was growing up I didn't even know there was such a thing."

"Do you use any kind of device to aid you?" I asked. "Not at the moment," Mehta said, "but as I grow older and injuries take longer to heal, I might well start using a cane. There's a real shift in the way I think about some of these problems. When I was younger, perhaps I had contempt for people who had to rely on the cane. But now I will use whatever helps me to function. If a time should come that I lose my hearing as well, I might use a seeing-eye dog, too.

"But there are so many ways in which you can be independent. Independence is a matter of the spirit."

A matter of habit, too, one might add. Mehta prefers a manual typewriter to his electric simply because he learned on a manual and is more comfortable with it. And "since most of my work is in the print media, I don't find much use for my Braille typewriter. But I certainly use it when I need to. For instance, if I'm going to make a speech, I'll make notes in Braille so that I can look them over in the middle of the night."

Mehta prefers to write by dictation, to an amanuensis who types his texts, then reads them back to him for revision. "My books have all been written, really, to be read aloud, because I write by sound. I think a lot of writers, even those who don't dictate, write by sound."

He acknowledges that technology has advanced so much that computers and tape recorders could be a boon to him, as they are to me. "I really think we should be thankful for anything that enhances a person's ability to function better. It probably would improve the speed of certain functions if I mastered computers, but it's just pure laziness that I don't."

There's no need to learn a new technology to help feed his family, for three years ago he won a MacArthur Foundation "genius" award of $236,000. For the next few years it will pay the rent and let him get on with the next volume of his memoirs, which will cover his college years at Pomona.

One thing that can't be aided by a cane, guide dog, computer or recorder is Mehta's astonishing memory. How is he able to reconstruct his life, including entire conversations, in such detail?

"I don't understand much about memory—I don't think even psychologists do. But for me it works by a process of free association. When I sat down to write this book I said to myself, 'What do I remember about arriving in New York City for the first time?' I thought I would remember nothing at all. But when I began writing, I asked myself, 'Which airport did I come in at? Who received me? How did I spend that first day?' As I wrote, things I didn't know I remembered came to the surface. I sometimes think that a human being forgets nothing. It's all stored there," he said, tapping his head.

"It's a matter of jarring the memory. I was helped by the letters I'd saved and carbon copies of letters I'd written. I'd kept a journal in Arkansas. I'm something of a pack rat." Mehta had thought *Sound-Shadows* would be a short book, he said, or just a chapter in another volume. But as he wrote, more and more memories surfaced, "and in the end it was a matter of cutting. I threw away lots and lots of material."

One of the memories he kept was one of rejection. He had hoped to attend the famous Perkins Institution for the Blind in Massachusetts, but they turned down the Indian boy because they feared he would be a "cultural misfit."

Arkansas, which trained blind youngsters in such things as basket-weaving, was willing to give him a try. But would Mehta's life have been different if he had gone to the more sophisticated school?

"When I was in college we used to play a game," he replied. "What if Napoleon had won at Waterloo? What if Charles Martel had not defeated the Muslims at Tours? If Napoleon had won, would all Englishmen be speaking French today? If Martel had lost, would all Europe be Muslim today?

"It's possible that given the sketchy education I had in India, I might have failed at Perkins. The truth of the matter is that in Arkansas, although the facilities and academic education were poor, I did learn something there that perhaps I wouldn't have learned so well at Perkins. That is mobility—getting around."

And, he added, the rustic Arkansas school was a "great democratic society. When you're a foreigner with a sketchy knowledge of English, that helped me a lot. Here in the backwoods were decent, hardworking, giving people who took a chance on me. They had no idea what would be involved, and they did the best they could.

"My affection for the place doesn't cloud my judgment about its inadequacies, but if it weren't for Arkansas I might be sitting back in India without the education I subsequently received."

If Mehta had remained in India, where education for the blind in those first years after independence was decidedly lacking, what would have happened?

He won't entertain the notion that he might have stayed. "There were practically no opportunities for the blind," he said, "and my father [a high government health official] had been trying to get me out since I was seven. A head of steam had built up over the years. Sooner or later I would have got out. Whether I would have got out in time to get the education I had—I don't know. I think of education as a form of liberation of the spirit, just as I think of mobility in the same way. Maybe I would have felt that I was under a prison sentence. In India, I felt as if I were in a cage. That's how I thought of blindness in those days.

"Being able to go to the West and be educated both here and in England freed my spirit, which makes the handicap under which I live much less cumbersome than it otherwise would have been. I think I was always outward bound, and if I were 15 today I would still be outward bound."

Outward bound: That's a good metaphor for the life of a man who is no less remarkable for his attitude as well as his accomplishments. It sounds like the serenity that comes with looking back on a rich and productive life, but it also may be the equanimity that comes from a mature acceptance of circumstance.

A few weeks before, I had overheard two people talking about me. One called me "the *Sun-Times'* deaf book editor." That irked me, for deafness is not part of the way I define myself. Doesn't it also irritate Mehta when people call him "the blind *New Yorker* writer"?

"As I grow older it matters very little

what people think or say," he replied. "You can't change what people think of you. People are what they are.

"But a time comes when you're defined by what you've done. People don't consider that 'the deaf Beethoven' wrote the Ninth Symphony or that 'the blind Milton' wrote the later poems. It's a matter of what you achieve at the end of the road."

Not long after writing this interview in 1985, I began to view myself in a different fashion. I was less judgmental about how the deaf looked to the hearing. And no longer did I worry so much about how other people felt about me; no longer did I bristle at their insistence on classifying me first as deaf and second as a journalist. I was no longer quite so hypersensitive about my speech, no longer so concerned about appearing stumbling, confused, and even retarded (as many hearing people unconsciously treat the deaf, even the deaf who are professional journalists). Ved Mehta was right. Let others believe what they chose. How I defined myself was more important. I was Henry Kisor, book editor and literary critic, husband and father, son and brother. "Deaf man" brought up the caboose of that train of self-characterization.

Ego-shoring recognition had begun to come my way, in the form of a clutch of plaques and awards from newspaper and literary groups, a few lines in *Who's Who in America*, and, one year, a nomination as a finalist for the Pulitzer Prize in criticism. The honor that meant the most to me, however, was an informal poll by the Northwestern University student newspaper that named me one of the most popular teachers on campus.

It had happened in 1982, when I had last stood at a lectern in musty old Fisk Hall, home of Northwestern's Medill School of Journalism, five years after beginning a moonlighting career there as an adjunct instructor. While we were still at the *Daily News*, a fellow *Panorama* staffer who taught Basic Writing—the intensive course in journalistic composition required of all Medill freshmen—suggested that I might have something of value to pass on to students. That appealed to my own school-masterish instincts.

It shouldn't be difficult, he explained. Each section of Basic Writing was small, typically no more than a dozen students, so that the instructor could give each freshman a great deal of attention. It was not a lecture course in a cavernous hall but an evening laboratory in a small classroom, with a type-writer at each desk.

The notion of teaching was so appealing that it temporarily buried my old phobia against speaking out in a group of strangers. I didn't think of it at all until half an hour before the first class was to begin. Then my heart started to pound, bullets of sweat sprang from my forehead, and my mouth dried into a desert. Hands shaking, coffee slopping from my cup, I stood before the freshmen and began in a high, quavering voice.

That evening luck smiled upon me. The members of the section were among the best and brightest in their class, curious and ex-pectant young people who seemed to assume that the man with the strange speech must have something of value to impart to them —otherwise he would not be standing before them. As I realized they understood what I said, my intestinal butterflies fluttered down and folded their wings.

Soon I happened upon the best strategy for teaching the class. Though it wasn't a lecture program but a hands-on course, Basic

Writing required fifteen minutes or so of preliminary remarks that included an explanation of the objectives of the evening's lesson and quotations from samples of writing, good and bad. At the best of times I'm not able to sustain enough precision in my speech, especially in extended talks, for unfamiliar listeners to understand more than 90 percent of it.

To my rescue came the electronic copier. Before each class I prepared a typed essay containing the evening's remarks, lesson objectives, and samples and ran off enough copies so that each student could have one. As I read from the remarks, the students would follow me with their copies. Often many of them would listen intently to my talk, referring to their copies only when a bungled phrase or sentence confused them. I exacted a quid pro quo from my students: if I took the trouble to give them copies of my remarks, they were responsible for taking the contents to heart.

I also tried hard to write as exhaustive a critique as I could of each student's work, in part because I never could get a lively class discussion going, for reasons I'm not quite certain about. Possibly the students felt I couldn't follow the bouncing ball of classroom conversation and therefore were disinclined to volley it back and forth. Maybe I simply couldn't light their fires, although they did give me their undivided attention whenever I spoke. In any event, I figured I would make up for this lack with a hand-written, sometimes typed, personal analysis and mini-lecture clipped to each story each student handed in, praising and cajoling where I could, trying to whet their enthusiasm for the hard work of writing well. It was time-consuming, but the technique seemed as efficient as that of any other instructor. In the end the experience was so satisfying that teaching is now part of my dream for the future: to spend the last decade or so of my career at a university somewhere in the Rocky Mountains that Debby and I love.

I left Medill for one simple reason: part-time salaries were tiny. Inflation was rampant at the time, Colin was just four years away from college, and I had begun another moonlighting career, as a columnist on personal computers. It was more lucrative than teaching.

During the summer of 1982 I bought an Osborne 1, a sewing-machine-sized portable that was the first affordable personal computer for many Americans. I wanted to do some freelance writing at home, and the swift and efficient word-processing system at the paper had spoiled me forever for typewriters. Like so many writers who discovered the personal computer at that time, I fell head over heels in love with the technology and even became messianic about it.

I persuaded my superiors at the *Sun-Times* that this machine would save our declining civilization and that it was their duty to allow me to bring the Word to the needy masses. They thought the proposal noble, but worth just $100 a week. Still, it was a beginning. Within a year I had syndicated the column to half a dozen other newspapers from Seattle and Los Angeles to Orlando, Florida. Colin's college fund soon grew healthy.

Of course, much of the great personal computer "revolution" was poorly disguised public relations hype, and I am afraid that in my unblinking enthusiasm I contributed a good deal to the fervent drivel written about it. But after the mid-1980s, when the industry matured, the journalists who covered it became more healthily skeptical about its potential, and I was no different. The column ended not long after the bloom wore off the "revolution," but I still occasionally write about the technology for computer magazines and for the *Sun-Times*'s book section, where from time to time a new item of word-processing software or hardware seems useful enough to merit a column on "Computing for Writers."

Amid all the fluff and nonsense, however, the coming of the personal computer truly revolutionized my life as a deaf person, not just as a writer. It enabled me to reach out to hearing people in ways I had never dreamed of.

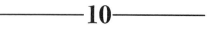

10

If one must be hearing-impaired, one couldn't choose a better time and place than the last two decades of the twentieth century in the United States. Thanks to a broad awakening of public consciousness about the rights and potentials of handicapped people, it's *easier* to be hearing-impaired today than at any other time in history. Not that deafness will ever be a convenience, but things could be much worse.

Two thousand years ago the Romans gave full rights only to the deaf who could either speak or read and write. The great majority—those who were deaf, speechless, and illiterate—had few privileges. That half loaf did result in the success of some deaf people, such as Quintus Pedius, whom Pliny considered one of the most eminent painters of Rome. (Quintus was the grandson of the consul of the same name who was co-heir to the will of Julius Caesar. Then, as now, coming from the right family never hurt anyone.)

All the deaf lost their rights during the Dark Ages, when the Church forbade them to receive communion because they could not confess their sins. Only in the fifteenth century, after the German scientist Agricola had discovered and celebrated a deaf and speechless man who had learned to read and write, did Europeans again accept the idea that those who could not speak or hear could be elevated to literacy. During the next century the Benedictine monk Pablo Ponce de León claimed success in teaching deaf Spanish aristocrats to speak, read, and write. There is considerable evidence that he did so by first teaching the children to write— an idea that would have pleased Doris Mirrielees immensely.

All that has undergone a sea change. In the United States today, a great deal of thought is being given to different ways of teaching the deaf to communicate and to help them take their rightful places in society. Thanks to such upheavals as the one at Gallaudet University in 1988, the deaf are even beginning to take their future into their own hands. They are aided by federal and state equal-access and entitlement laws that have established public funding of sign language interpreters for the deaf who need them in courtrooms, hospitals, schools, and other public institutions. Private organizations for the hearing-impaired often provide interpreters for social occasions. In some states, it's common—even unremarkable—for interpreters to attend lectures with deaf students at hearing colleges, for the law requires federally funded agencies such as schools and hospitals to provide them. The same laws give deaf people with hearing-ear dogs the same rights of access to hotels, restaurants, and public transportation as the blind with seeing-eye dogs. Equal-opportunity statutes are designed to ensure that the deaf get a fair shake at employment.

In practical terms, most of these things haven't been of great benefit to me, except in the general awakening they've encouraged, both in the United States and abroad. People do seem to be a bit more patient and understanding today; in fact, I am often struck that strangers frequently react without surprise to my announcement of deafness. Thanks in great part to the publicity the mass media have given the world of the deaf in recent years, it's rare to encounter the kind of thoughtless ignorance that makes a deaf person feel as if he is being treated like a pitiable subhuman.

Young people especially seem to accept the deaf as something more than "weirdos," possibly because so many deaf youngsters are being mainstreamed in public schools. I'm often startled and gratified when a perky teenaged fast-food server takes my order, then smiles, looks me in the eye, and repeats the order, not in a painfully exaggerated way, but slowly enough so that I can understand readily.

Others who serve the public—salespeople and waiters, ticket agents and bus drivers, police officers and vendors—also seem to be much less taken aback by the idea of dealing with a deaf person, especially one who communicates with them in their own fashion. All in all, I don't feel as conspicuous as I used to whenever I open my mouth in public. And the little confrontations of each day don't seem quite so daunting anymore. Occasionally they do happen, but I've learned simply to brush them off, or perhaps add them to my store of anecdotes on the sometimes amusing, sometimes vexing pitfalls of lipreading. It is a wonderful knack to have, and it will always get me through the day, but at times its inadequacies try my soul.

One evening not long ago, for instance, a plainclothes policeman loomed in the front doorway of my home. He displayed his shield and asked sternly, "Did you buy gasoline today?"

"Yes," I replied, startled. Then, because it's always good sense when dealing with officials of any kind, I added the customary announcement: "Officer, I'm deaf, but I can read lips." The cop was courteous but blunt. "The attendant at the station where you bought the gas," he said, clearly enunciating each word, "says she gave you too much change—five dollars—and you ran off with it."

"She did not and I did not!" I replied indignantly. With a sinking feeling, however, I realized that I'd often been careless about counting change. That afternoon the attendant had handed back a few bills and coins, which I didn't bother to check, and she had added what I thought was the ubiquitous "Thank you. Have a nice day." I had smiled back, walked out to the car, and drove off—while she called the police with my license number.

"Uh . . . she may have," I told the cop. "She said something I didn't understand."

"Let's go talk to the fellow who owns the station," said the policeman, who by this time had sized up the situation. Evanston policemen have become knowledgeable about deafness, for there are quite a few hearing-impaired people in the community. "You understand you're not under arrest?" he asked solicitously as we walked out to his cruiser. I nodded, hoping the neighbors peering from their windows understood, too.

At the gas station I shamefacedly explained what had happened. The owner, a bit embarrassed himself, replied that his attendant had been "ripped off once too often and had wanted to nail a thief, even for a lousy five dollars." He wasn't sufficiently abashed to refuse the money I proffered.

When we returned to my house and the five-dollar desperado alighted from the police car, the cop leaned out the window and said with a thin smile, "Next time, count your change."

And next time you don't catch the words, I told myself ruefully, ask the person to repeat what was said . . . even if it turns out to be a ubiquitous inanity such as "Have a good one." Of course, I haven't kept that part of the resolution, at least not with store clerks, for life is too short to waste on polite noises. Someday, I'm certain, I'll be found out again. But now I always count my change.

Each year I spend a week or two in Europe or the Far East on assignment for the *Sun-Times*'s travel section, usually with a group of journalists but sometimes on my own. I'm often surprised at how nonchalant European restaurateurs and hoteliers are about deaf people as guests. (Their American colleagues certainly aren't clumsy about it, but it often takes a Manhattan or Los Angeles desk clerk a brief instant to recover from the surprise.) Often I have to awaken at an early hour to depart for my next destination, and when I explain to foreign desk managers that I am deaf and cannot receive a wake-up phone call, they're quick to understand that a bell-hop must be sent to my room at the appointed hour to unlock the door and turn on the lights to rouse me. I leave the night latch off not only for this purpose but also so that someone can get into the room in case of fire. I am less afraid of burglars than I am of burning to death.

Just once, in Rome, did I have a problem. It was a brand-new hotel and, while the clerks' English was not as bad as my Italian, they simply could not seem to understand why they could not telephone me to awaken me. I didn't have the Italian for "I can't hear *anything*. I'm stone deaf, deaf as a post, deaf as a whatever the Romans say." Only when a passing scrublady, who evidently had heard our confused exchange, spoke up did light finally dawn on the clerks.

I've often found that Europeans understand even the most wretched accent in their own languages better than they do Deaf American English. "Have you got a laundry service?" I once repeatedly asked a Paris desk clerk. He peered at me in concerned puzzlement, trying hard to achieve a breakthrough, but just couldn't. But when I pulled out my American Express phrase book, riffled to the right page, and recited, *"Y a-t-il une blanchisserie?"* a bright and benign light of understanding swept over his countenance, and he replied, *"Oui.* Just drop eet off here in ze morning."

Just once or twice have I needed rescue from official misunderstanding in a foreign land. One day on Barbados, Debby and I had just debarked from a cruise ship and were waiting for our luggage to clear dockside customs so that we could hail a taxi for the airport and return to the United States. An arrogant customs agent kept us cooling our heels while she alternated long, lazy pulls from a cigarette and a bottle of beer in her office. Time shortened, and we grew nervous about missing our plane. Finally the agent emerged from her office, and I waved anxiously. She sauntered over and said, "Have you anything to declare?"

I did not understand—it may have been her unfamiliar Barbadian accent—and hesitated. Immediately her eyes glittered with scorn and triumph. She raised her arm, pointed an accusing finger, and (Debby said later) bellowed, "This man doesn't know if he has anything to declare!"

As I peered confusedly at the agent, visions of roach-infested Caribbean jails marched across Debby's mind. She immediately shouted back, "My husband is deaf! He didn't understand what you said!" Her vehemence flustered the agent, who immediately passed our luggage without examining it, as if to get rid of an unwelcome embarrassment, and Debby hustled it and me out of the customs shed into a taxi. We made our plane with moments to spare.

Later I told Debby in a wounded tone that I thought I could have handled the situation. "Yes," she replied soothingly, "but by the time you got everything straightened out we'd have missed the plane."

But I had my revenge. As we approached U.S. customs at Kennedy Airport, she said,

"Now let me handle this." "No, let *me* handle it," I insisted, dragging our luggage to the agent at the counter. Handing him our passports, I pointed to my ear, looked woebegone, and said, "I'm deaf." Not my usual brisk and businesslike "I'm deaf, but I read lips," but a slow and desolate "I'm de-e-e-af." (If I'd thought of it, I would have limped and scuttled like Igor.)

With a nod and smile—and no questions—the customs agent waved us through. That was, it appeared, easier for him than struggling to communicate with a deaf man. I could have smuggled in a fortune in diamonds. American immigration and customs agents almost always assume I'm above reproach once I announce my deafness. Europeans, however, take nothing for granted, and the single time I passed through Tokyo a cadre of white-gloved agents answered me by carefully examining every shirt, sock, and shoe in my luggage.

Now, when dealing with immigration and customs agents of any nationality, I make sure they know I can't hear. I'm proud of my independence, but in commerce with bureaucrats it's smarter to avoid the game of seeing how long I can go without letting the other fellow know I'm deaf. (Sometimes, especially if I have no difficulty understanding people, they just think my gravelly and nasal deaf man's speech is the result of a dolorous bout with the grippe, and the game can go on for a surprisingly long time.)

The most unpleasant traveling experience I have ever had occurred at home, aboard an Amtrak train from Chicago to New York, and I'm not certain what, if anything, anyone could have done to prevent it. On this trip I was traveling alone in a sleeping-car roomette, whose door cannot be opened from the outside if it is locked from the inside. Too much shaking, rattling, and rolling goes on aboard a train for me to feel the vibrations of a knock at the door, and I always pulled the roomette or bedroom door to but left it unlocked in case a conductor knocked. A deaf person never can lock himself off completely from the outside world. In an emergency there has to be a way for someone to get in to announce the presence of danger.

This time I awakened from a sound sleep with an uncomfortable sensation in my posterior, as if I were perching on a fence post. I looked up and saw that light was spilling from the corridor into the roomette. Then I raised myself on my elbows and looked around. A dark shape was leaning into the roomette, its hand underneath the blankets. I was being groped.

With an angry cry I sprang into a sitting position and unleashed a haymaker that missed its target by yards and catapulted me into the opposite wall. I scrambled out into the corridor to give chase to the groper, fast disappearing into the next car, but realized I was in my underwear, and halted. After checking to see that my wallet and belongings were intact, I gave up the idea of reporting the incident to the conductor. I hadn't gotten a good look at the culprit and would never have been able to identify him.

It is not only the elevating of public consciousness about the hearing-impaired that has freed us from centuries of isolation. For many of us the microchip is probably the greatest aid to communication the twentieth century has yet provided. It has made possible hearing aids of sophistication, miniaturization, and power unheard of in the days when I toted that heavy Bakelite brick and its batteries in a harness. It has led to medical advances such as cochlear implants, tiny devices that when surgically placed within the inner ear help certain hearing-impaired patients to overcome the greatest frustrations of soundlessness.

The microchip has also made possible inexpensive, small, noiseless, durable, and easily obtainable replacements for the huge, clattering old teletype machines that a generation ago first allowed deaf people to "talk" with one another on the telephone. Today's TDD—short for "Telecommunications Device for the Deaf"—looks like a lightweight portable typewriter with a keyboard and two rubber cups into which a telephone handset is inserted. It's simply a computerized version of the teletype, its eight-inch-wide roll-paper printer replaced by an electronic digital readout that displays a single glowing line of text. (Some TDDs can also print out text on narrow cash-register paper.)

All deaf residents of Illinois are now entitled to a free TDD, thanks to a five-cent-a-month charge applied to all phone bills in the state. Most government offices, libraries, and other public institutions also have TDDs. Partly as an exercise in corporate noblesse oblige and partly to win the business of deaf people, a growing number of private firms are installing the machines and publicizing their phone numbers.

Why not? A TDD does not tie up a phone line. The device sits unobtrusively next to the phone until it's needed. It's easy to tell when a call from a TDD is coming in; the caller presses its space bar repeatedly, sending distinctive beeps. And no training is required to operate the machine; one simply turns it on, places the telephone handset into the rubber cups, and taps away on the keyboard.

In the early 1980s, when the telephone companies first began renting TDDs to the deaf for a low monthly charge and to businesses and institutions for a bit more, I persuaded the *Sun-Times* to try an inexpensive three-month experiment: renting a TDD for me at the office while I obtained another for home. At the very least I'd be able to call home and talk with my family, just as my co-workers did. Perhaps, if the TDD became widely used, it would be a boon to me in other ways as well.

And it was. Before long I bought a lightweight, book-sized, battery-operated portable TDD that I could take on the road, calling from phone booths and hotel rooms to my home or even to the paper, where I'd arrange for another editor to keep the office TDD by her desk in case I should call. The

307

Sun-Times pronounced the experiment successful and kept the TDD.

I've used TDDs to make airline and hotel reservations and to call public libraries to obtain information about authors. Every other week I use one to touch base with my parents in Pennsylvania; they bought a $200 TDD just to communicate with their deaf son eight hundred miles away. Being able to speak with each other without resorting to the aid of a third party is a mutual comfort. And now my son Colin has my old portable TDD with him at college, and calls home occasionally for a father-son shmooze.

As for reaching people who might not deal with enough deaf customers to warrant owning or renting a TDD—dentists and doctors as well as pizza parlors come to mind—deaf communities in many cities have organized "relay stations" of hearing volunteers, many of them physically handicapped and housebound. These volunteers take TDD calls from the deaf and relay them by voice to their destinations, then call the TDD users back with the responses. Now that access to a TDD has become the right of every deaf person in Illinois, the state is beginning to organize and finance professional relay systems. Some states, such as California, already have well-developed relay systems with two phone lines, one for the TDD and the other for voice, so that no call-backs are needed. Within a few years, thanks to legislation pending before Congress at this writing, a network of relay systems is likely to crisscross the United States.

TDDs indeed have opened a wide door on the closed world of the deaf, helping end a great deal of its isolation. But for the time being, TDDs are still specialized devices for handicapped users. They're not the kind of appliance one finds in every home or business; their use is still limited to a tiny portion of the American population. And for technical reasons, due to their teletypewriter heritage, they are slow. It's easy for a fast typist to outrun a TDD's transmission rate; when that happens, the message becomes garbled and unreadable.

The personal computer has revolutionized not only my professional but my personal life as well. When I bought that Osborne 1 in 1982, it was intended strictly as a writing machine. But before long I added to my system a modem, a device that allows two computers to exchange information over the phone. It allowed me to transmit articles and columns written at home on the Osborne to the big mainframe computer at the *Sun-Times* so that I would not have to retype them at the office.

But there are other uses for a modem. Soon I discovered that I could use it to communicate with other people—*hearing* people. The vehicle is the electronic bulletin board system—"BBS," for short. These are personal computers, owned by hobbyists, that employ modems and special software to turn themselves into glorified answering machines for other computers. One can call a BBS with one's own computer and modem, and then type in a password in order to read messages, public and private, other people have left on the system. The best analogue for a BBS is a kind of electronic rural general store. People drop in from all over to set a spell, picking up gossip with their video screens and passing on their own chitchat with their keyboards. They can even "talk" with the proprietor of the system, taking turns typing away at their keyboards, their sentences following one another on-screen.

It wasn't long before I figured out that all one needed to "keyboard-talk" with another computer user was ordinary modem software on the computers at both ends of the phone line. At prearranged times I could call a fellow computer user and "chat" with him. This is very much like using a TDD, but without the technical problems. Computers are much faster than TDDs; even the fastest typist can't outrun a computer's transmission rate. And the large screen of the computer is much more efficient than the TDD's single-line display.

Most important, the personal computer and modem are universal appliances, not special devices associated with a particular handicap, as TDDs are for the deaf. For the first time, they enabled me to "talk" on the phone with the *hearing* world at large—with fellow members of my own culture. To me they were truly an instrument of liberation.

Before long I discovered that these computer conversations need not be expensive long-distance calls, either. They can be conducted through organizations called videotex services that maintain phone connections in cities everywhere. These services are by day large computer database services for business and industry, and by night information exchanges for computer hobbyists. For an hourly charge (twelve to fifteen dollars is typical) plus the cost of a local call, personal computer users can call up a videotex service, send "electronic mail" to other subscribers around the country, and pick up their own. They can also make use of a feature called "Chat," in which hundreds of computer users around the country and in foreign lands can "talk" simultaneously with their keyboards. The conversation can be a giant free-for-all like a citizens band radio colloquy, or a private one-to-one conversation, or a "conference call" limited to two, three, or more persons.

For me, computer-chatting was a staggering revolution in communications. For the first time I could participate in group talks without worrying about whether people could understand my speech, whether they would listen to what I had to say rather than how I said it, and whether I could follow the bouncing ball of conversation among a large number of people.

Wholeheartedly I plunged into it, spending hours every evening in electronic chats with people all over the country. Debby became a computer widow, my children orphans. I was oblivious to their loneliness. For I was meeting many, many fascinating people. An emergency-room physician in Memphis shared my love for Gerard Manley Hopkins' verse. A young novelist in Cleveland related his agonizing experiences trying to break into print. A Chicago psychologist told of her work with convicts. A Texas housewife confided the secrets of setting up a successful home-based word-processing business. A sheriff's policeman in Georgia told fascinating stories about law enforcement among the deaf. It was like a giant electronic town meeting, with people from all walks of life plunging into swirling currents of conversation. If one tired of public chatter, one could enter a few commands to talk privately with one or two others. I reveled in it.

After the first blush of novelty wore off, drawbacks appeared. Videotex chatting tends to attract unpleasant insects—juveniles and emotionally deprived adults eager for sexual conversations (or "interactive porn") as well as poseurs pretending to be wealthy and accomplished people. Yet most computer-chatters are perfectly normal people who take occasional pleasure in this form of communication. Some regular users suffer from physical defects that keep them housebound and have few other ways to interact with fellow humans. But persistent sociopaths abound on-line, and it is sometimes difficult to shake them off.

And when all is said and done, computer communication is really no substitute for regularly interacting in the flesh with other human beings—and I'm no hermit.

Moreover, that hourly charge can easily run up enormous bills, especially if one plunges into computer-chatting with any regularity. After receiving several staggering invoices, I looked for a cheaper way to connect with my computer chums, especially those around the Chicago area. The answer was to set up an electronic bulletin board of my own. Anyone with a personal computer and a modem could phone my system and leave a message or "beep" me for a live keyboard chat. When I was at home, the ringing modem would flash a lamp to alert me to a call.

By late 1984 I'd bought another computer, a more powerful IBM-compatible, for my syndicated column on personal computers, and the Osborne was lying largely unused. Why not, I thought, use the Osborne for a BBS with public-domain bulletin-board software free for the taking? But I was no programmer; I knew how to use word-processing programs and that was all. One needed to be a sophisticated hobbyist to set up a bulletin board. Help eventually came from a friend who operated a BBS on his Osborne as a hobby. His spouse was hearing-impaired, so he had a natural interest in helping deaf people. Swiftly he customized his software for my use, and a new avenue of communication lay open for me.

Today, with a lightweight laptop computer, I can "phone home" to the BBS, pick up my messages, and talk with my family from the office or from hotel rooms when I'm on the road. When I'm at the office, I load the laptop with BBS software so that Debby can call me at the office from *her* computer at home. So can a host of friends and colleagues, some of them writers and reviewers. If I happen to be away from my desk when they call, they can leave messages. This world is still narrow, for people who enjoy communicating by computer tend to be hobbyists rather than the ordinary public. As time goes on, however, such equipment is likely to become cheaper, simpler to use, and as ubiquitous as an ordinary telephone.

For the larger world of the deaf, though, computers are still impractical for telephone communications. They're expensive, and most people in the deaf community, who earn far less on the average than the hearing, can't afford even the three or four hundred dollars a well-used, obsolescent computer might cost. Many who speak only American Sign Language, whose syntax bears little relation to that of English, feel uncomfortable attempting to keyboard-chat with hearing people in an unfamiliar language. For them and many others, TDDs are a better choice.

Another revolutionary electronic device that has made a large difference in my life as well as in the lives of almost all other deaf people is the closed-caption decoder. That's a small "black box" plugged between the antenna and the TV set which transforms encoded electronic signals from television transmitters into captions on the screen, much like subtitles on foreign films. Without the decoder, unneeded captions don't clutter up the sets of hearing people. Thus the system is called "closed" captioning.

The television networks send videotapes of their shows to captioning specialists such as the National Captioning Institute in Falls Church, Virginia. There hearing listeners transcribe the dialogue on the tapes and encode it into captions on magnetic discs. The discs are then sent to the networks, where the caption signals are inserted electronically into the television picture, then transmitted along with the normal audio and video portions of the program.

The closed captioner first appeared in 1980 and since then has become the greatest electronic entertainment aid the deaf have ever had. Before it came along, even expert lipreaders had a hard time puzzling out what the "talking heads" were saying on the two-dimensional television screen. Voice-over narration deepened the fog.

I could easily follow only sports events. Movies were difficult unless I'd read the books on which they were based—if there were any. Talky British drawing-room dramas such as those showcased on *Masterpiece Theatre* might as well have been in Urdu for all I could understand of them. As for dramas and situation comedies, only shows with a lot of action were halfway comprehensible, and I'd have to fill in the gaps with my own imagination, inventing plot and dialogue to match the movements on-screen. The resulting "scenarios" often merely lampooned the genuine versions, as I would learn later, when the captioners came along. Often I'd prefer my fantasies to the real ones. That's no tribute to my imagination but a measure of the clay-footedness of American television programming.

Today almost all prime-time network shows are captioned, and PBS captions the majority of its evening programs. Though local news broadcasts are captioned in many cities, only in the last year have two Chicago stations captioned their news. Each year, however, the number of closed-captioned shows grows.

The captions are not encoded verbatim. An actor might say, "Baby, how's about you and me making a little whoopee?" But the caption instead might read: "Baby, let's make love." This foreshortening is done for two reasons. First, there might not be room on the screen to display a long-winded bit of dialogue, even in successive fragments. Second, on the average deaf viewers read more slowly than people speak, so some shrinking of dialogue is necessary for it to be displayed on-screen long enough for the viewers to read it.

Many of the spices and subtleties of language thus are lost. In the early days of closed captioning, for example, the plummy locutions of upper-class British English gave way to Standard Blandspeak in captions prepared for BBC imports on American public television. As time has gone on, however, the captioning companies evidently have determined that deaf viewers who tune in to PBS shows tend to be better educated and more sophisticated than those who watch commercial network television, and thus the captions can follow the actual dialogue more closely.

Then there is live, or "real-time," closed captioning, performed on the fly by human transcribers with the help of computers, much like court reporters. In this manner all three commercial networks live-caption their news, their coverage of presidential addresses, and even some sports events. Live captioning is still in the process of development, and at times can be primitive—even hilarious. "Pulitzer Prize" might be rendered "pullet surprise," and one morning an ABC weatherman advised his viewers, according to the captions, to "drivel carefully." And fresh names and concepts in the news often are garbled unrecognizably until the proper spellings can be fed into the computer's lexicon. There is also necessarily a delay between the spoken word and the appearance of the caption on-screen. The video might switch to the wreckage of a plane crash while the captions are still discussing a political event.

But I'm not complaining. No longer do I have to wait until the next day to read the text of a presidential address in *The New York Times*. I do, however, turn off the captioner during *Monday Night Football*. Who needs the inane, clichéd chatter of pro football commentators? Silence can sometimes be a blessing.

Closed captions are also being recorded on films released in videocassette. Many recent movies are captioned at the same time they are released as videos, and more and more classic old films have been re-released with captions. These enable the deaf to participate in an important segment of popular culture that in the past largely had been lost to them. One Saturday not long ago I rented *Gone With the Wind*. I'd known about Rhett Butler's famous "Frankly, my dear, I don't give a damn," but it was the first I'd heard of Scarlett's "Fiddle-de-dee!"

A little-known side benefit of captioned videos is as a "language lab" for lipreaders. Watching the lips of the speakers at the instant the captions appear on-screen will sharpen the skills of any speechreader. It's not long before one begins to understand all the words the captions leave out. And it's excellent practice in accustoming oneself to non-American accents. After years of watching *Masterpiece Theatre* as well as scores of captioned British films, I've discovered that on trips to the United Kingdom I have much less trouble lipreading most Britons. Even cockneys aren't the puzzle they used to be.

One final electronic device should be mentioned: the cochlear implant. This is a tiny network of wires embedded surgically in the cochlea of the ear which send impulses to the auditory nerve. Electrical impulses from a microphone worn on the body carry sound from the outside into this network, enabling the patient to feel sensations in his ears very much like hearing. *Is* it hearing? There is a good deal of argument about that.

As the technique has advanced, the number of implanted wires increases the range of frequencies that can be "felt" through the auditory nerve. Newspaper reports have claimed that with these implants people who have lost their hearing to nerve deafness can again understand speech without lipreading. But this seems to be an exaggeration. Those who benefit from it most tend to do so psychologically. The gross sounds they hear give them more confidence than understanding.

Quite recently, after reading news stories on advances in implant technique, I investigated the possibility of undergoing it myself. But I was turned down without even an interview, because I had lost my hearing at what the surgeons considered too early an age. They said I could no longer remember what hearing was like, and therefore would be a poor subject for the arduous training required after the surgery. The patient has to learn to "hear"—if that is the word—all over again.

A wise audiology professor at Northwestern University pointed out that I was already light-years ahead in dealing with my deafness compared with those considered the best prospects for cochlear surgery—those who had lost their hearing later in life, when adjustment to the loss was at its most difficult. "Why interfere with what already works?" he said sensibly.

Indeed, Dean Garstecki is a veritable model of sensibility. I met him several years ago, when I realized that my speech was again beginning to deteriorate and that I needed some brush-up therapy if I was to maintain it at a reasonable level of intelligibility. I wrote a note to a friend at the Chicago Hearing Society, on whose board of directors I had briefly served a few years before. Could she put me in touch with someone who could help?

To my surprise she suggested my old battleground, the Institute of Language Disorders at Northwestern—now called the Department of Communication Sciences and Disorders. The prospect did not fill me with joy, but I reasoned that I had nothing to lose, and perhaps a different philosophy had displaced the irritating old paternalism, even arrogance, that I had experienced two and three decades before. Besides, private speech therapists cost a good deal of money.

Instantly Garstecki, head of the department's program in audiology and hearing impairment, lifted my concern. He wasn't interested in what went on in my head, he said. That was irrelevant. Clearly I'd made a good adjustment to life as a deaf person. Let's treat what obviously ails me—my speech. And so, for nearly a decade, I have spent a quarter or two of every other academic year as a client at the institute, brushing up on my "s"s and "e"s and learning to put the brakes on so that I don't runmywordsalltogetherlikethis.

In the beginning I had hoped to improve my speech to a silver-tongued point, one that would allow me to orate before large groups of hearing strangers. From time to time I am invited to lecture on literary topics, a task that can be lucrative. Perhaps after hours a day of intensive training over many months, the quality of my speech could be raised to a level close to that of the normal hearing person. Retaining that quality, however, might require just as much labor—a game that might not be worth the candle.

I cannot hear myself speak; my lips, tongue, mouth, and larynx may seem to me to be going through the correct motions to produce intelligible speech, but their synchronization may be off ever so much, my tongue and teeth not quite in the right position with the precise tension required to produce a certain sound properly. The difference between the right and the wrong placement of the structures of the mouth is very, very subtle, and I cannot always tell the difference.

The only way I can tell with any consistency if my speech is understandable is to watch the reaction of the strangers to whom I speak. If they knit their brows, or gaze at me vacantly, we're not connecting. It's when

I have to repeat myself more and more to be understood that I know my speech is slipping, that it's time to go back to Northwestern for a brush-up.

Our sessions do not seek dramatic breakthroughs. They are simply intended to maintain my intelligibility at a level somewhere above 90 percent—that is, a level at which a stranger talking to me for the first time would understand at least 90 percent of what I said. That might seem a modest goal, but it requires a lot of hard work and conscientious drilling at home. Once a week my therapist and I meet across a table in a small room for an hour. Our largest difficulty is finding some way for me to monitor the quality of my speech. We try, fail, try again, fail again, suddenly find the right placement, lose it, find it again, try to hang on to it, and sometimes succeed. Each session is a mixture of frustration, satisfaction, and sometimes elation.

"Hold that thought," say my therapists as I leave each session. At the bus stop on the way to work each morning, I peer around to see whether anyone's in earshot, then run through my drills, warming up for the day. To sharpen my "e"s, the vowel with which I have the most trouble—it often comes out too lax, almost like an "uh"—I'll concoct sentences full of "e"s. "Evil babies eat eels from the sea" is one of my favorites. Waiting for the bus one day, I reeled off a dozen shapely and orotund "evil babies" sentences, exaggerating that "e" so that the proper sound would stay with me all day even when I wasn't thinking about it. Then I looked around and saw that another commuter had joined me. She stared warily and kept her distance.

My instructors are graduate students training to be speech therapists, not teachers of the deaf. Most of the therapists are women less than half my age. They are still learning their specialty, and over the years I've often been amused by their transparent efforts to present a brisk, businesslike, professional image to their clients. They are so very young, and they look like freshly minted nickels in the dress-for-success suits they don for our sessions instead of the sweats and jeans they wear to class.

And they are eager and determined. The truly talented among them quickly lose their stiffness and help develop a rapport, joining me in what amounts to an eager, even gleeful conspiracy against unintelligibility. The very best therapists are single-minded and hard-nosed. They won't settle for a reasonable approximation of a sound; they demand perfection. I am capable of achieving it, they declare, and they won't be satisfied with less. And once in a while I do manage to attain that exalted level. Hanging on to it, of course, is something else, so I must go back now and again for routine maintenance, like an aging automobile in need of periodic tune-ups.

I am eternally grateful to these young almost-professionals, for the results always are worth the time spent in the sessions. For more than a year, sometimes two, strangers will understand what I say the first time I say it at our first meeting, the benchmark by which I judge my speech. Though I'm still aware of its limitations—raising my voice at noisy gatherings still distorts my production and hurts intelligibility—my speech feels solid enough to get me through most situations. In short, when it's running smoothly on all cylinders it gives me a confidence I haven't always had.

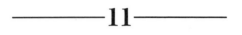

11

"Are you happy?" I was asked not long ago by someone who works in the world of the deaf.

I? I who have a loving spouse, two bright and strapping sons, a decent income, respect in my profession, a house in a pleasant suburb, and a host of good friends?

"Of course I am!" I all but shouted, exasperatedly throwing my hands into the air. I'm as happy as any other person whom life has nourished from a mixed plate of blessings and curses. It's difficult, however, to persuade some people that is true; they often assume that I am at heart forlorn and despondent, and concealing my pain. According to the ideology of many educators of the deaf—and many of the deaf themselves—I must live a melancholy life simply because I communicate wholly by speech and lip-reading rather than with sign language. By insisting on doing so, they declare, I am a poor shadow of a hearing person, not a contented and fulfilled deaf person. I belong neither to the hearing world nor to the deaf community, they say; I am an outcast from both.

Is the goal of life to become well adjusted and carefree? Or is it rather to rise high in a competitive world? These notions are not mutually exclusive—and it's a safe guess that most people, deaf or hearing, achieve a balance between the two. But it's sometimes hard to persuade naysayers that the deaf who choose the road of speech and lipreading can manage to achieve emotional equilibrium within the hearing world.

Partly because I have no measurable hearing—the deaf who succeed in the hearing world tend to have a good deal of residual hearing that can be amplified to usable levels—some experts on deafness insist on forcing me into the mold of the "deaf personality," a set of traits they theorize are created by the environment of deafness. Because lack of ready communication at an early age has deprived them of the opportunity to develop emotionally in many ways, the deaf sometimes are psychologically typed as immature, rigid, egocentric, impulsive, and overly trusting. And that's just for starters. If their emotional development has been severely thwarted, many suffer debilitating mental illness.

That deafness *has* affected my mental makeup I have no doubt. To deny it would be to declare that environment has no part in the development of the human psyche, and that would be absurd. Obviously there have been times in my life, in both my childhood and my adulthood, when a knowledgeable counselor could have helped me deal with a deep emotional crisis. But, as do most essentially healthy people faced with mental upheavals, I managed, with the help of Debby and my friends, to emerge from each crisis as a stronger and wiser human being.

There have been two crises in my adulthood, linked to one another, and one still must be contended with. That is shyness. It's almost universal among the deaf to want to cause hearing people as little fuss as possible; though there are exceptions, we can be self-effacing and diffident to the point of invisibility. Sometimes this tendency can be crippling. I must fight it all the time, and on occasion it can get the better of me.

I hate crowds, and I dislike meeting strangers. I will find any excuse not to undergo that exceedingly complex ordeal. Let's face it: it is natural and inevitable for hearing people to consider a new acquaintance's deafness the salient part of his personality. "This is a *deaf* person I am meeting," goes the unspoken question in the back of their minds, "and how is his deafness going to affect our relations?" Not the usual mildly expectant curiosity such as "This is Debby Kisor's husband I am meeting and will I like him for the same reasons I like her?"

If I'm lucky, I think, the person I am meeting will have no preconceived notions about the deaf. But that almost never happens. People bring to a meeting a lifetime's mental baggage. Some of it will be wise, some of it foolish, some of it astute, some of it ignorant. Sometimes their mental picture of the deaf will be a vague idea that they are extraordinarily difficult to communicate with, that because they cannot speak well they are not too bright but it is necessary to be kind. Fortunately this Neanderthal notion is rare and growing rarer.

In my experience most people are simply too ignorant about the deaf to consider them members of a somewhat slow subspecies of humanity. They will form their judgments upon our meeting, not before. Usually their judgments will be skewed, and it won't be their fault. Their problem—and mine—is one of communication, beginning with my imperfect speech. It takes time for a stranger to get accustomed to it, to feel comfortable enough with it so that he listens to what I have to say rather than how I say it. Likewise, I must "learn" the stranger's manner of speaking. If I'm lucky, he'll be instantly understandable. More often than not it'll take a few minutes before both of us stop saying "Would you please repeat that?"

Often, however, strangers won't ask me to repeat myself if they can't understand me. They're afraid of hurting my feelings. They don't realize that after forty-six years of deafness I'm no longer so embarrassed by my sometimes unintelligible speech. Irritated and frustrated, yes, but hardly devastated.

This social interaction, so simple between hearing people, becomes between the deaf and the hearing an intricate but curiously graceless ballet, like a Balanchine *pas de deux* choreographed on an off day. Realizing all this, I know that if an introduction is to be successful, it's up to me to meet the other person more than halfway, to put him at his ease. And when it's necessary, I will.

In his splendid 1972 autobiography, *Deafness,* the British poet David Wright opined that coping with another's deafness is an excellent "litmus test" of a hearing person's character. Those with inquiring, interested minds, he wrote, will want to learn the intricacies of a deaf person's life. The dull and self-absorbed, on the other hand, will be too fearful to risk the social awkwardness of meeting and talking with a deaf person. In many cases this is true, but it doesn't tell the whole story. The brilliant can be shy, and the kindly fearful of giving offense. If I let my deafness do the sorting out, I can be cheating myself of the chance to know someone worth knowing. So, for the most part, I will grit my teeth and plunge ahead into the chore of attempting to put the other person at his ease. More often than not, the experiment will work.

Much of the success of the ordeal of introduction depends upon where it is made. A quiet office or living room enables the introducee to encounter my speech and voice at its very best. As I've explained, background noise affects my intelligibility, most often at cocktail parties. Often the other person will be unable to hear me at all, let alone understand me, and turning up the volume on my larynx distorts certain sounds so badly that I am not intelligible at all. And if

I am tired, my speech—and my lipreading ability—will suffer. When this happens, I get cranky, mulish, and standoffish, proffering a perfunctory handshake and the shortest of polite noises. I know perfectly well I'm being silly, that I'm depriving myself of the potential to know someone interesting. "You're being unreasonable," Debby will hiss. "I know," I want to hiss back, "but, dammit, I can't help it."

Fortunately these episodes are infrequent. When it's necessary to meet someone, I'll set the stage as carefully as I can. Whether meeting a new neighbor or interviewing an author, I'll make sure the setting is quiet and undistracting. And if I can't do that, I'll try to wait until I can. Such are the little strategies of deafness.

Developing them took many years and a few wrong turns. One of those led to the second major personal crisis of my adult life: a flirtation with alcohol.

When I was a young man, I occasionally took on a few ounces of Dutch courage before and during social affairs. A couple of drinks eased the chore of talking to strangers at literary cocktail parties and on Friday nights at Ricardo's, a Chicago newspaperman's watering hole. Like so many other young journalists, I thought my life wasn't complete unless I joined the crowd for drunken bull sessions after a long, hard week.

Alcohol made me both braver and mellower, able to plunge into conversation more easily. It also, as one would expect, made me less intelligible. In the beginning my speech just would become slightly slurred, as it will for anyone with a few drinks under his belt. As the years went on, however, the slurring deepened as my tolerance for alcohol grew and I drank more to achieve that warm buzz of mellowness. The harder it became to understand me over the noise, the more I would drink. Soon came a point at many functions at which liquor was served when nobody could understand me at all. All that was left for me to do was stand by the bar, smiling idiotically and getting ever more befuddled.

I could easily have become a thoroughgoing alcoholic, and by some definitions of the term I'm sure I was. Usually I got inebriated just two or three Friday nights each month. Because I recovered by Monday morning, my work was never affected. But I would come home very late, sometimes not remembering how. One morning, after a literary gathering in New York, I woke up in a hotel room. My clothes lay neatly folded over a chair, my shoes aligned at the foot of the bed. But it wasn't the hotel I'd checked into the day before. My head pounding, I asked the desk clerk how much I owed. Nothing, he said. It had been paid for in cash the night before. I still do not remember how I got there or the name and face of the good Samaritan who must have paid the bill and put me to bed.

Such blackouts mean that a drinker is reaching a point of no return. Fortunately, I knew enough about alcoholism to become concerned about those lapses in memory, and not long after that episode Debby finally had enough of my staggering home in the wee hours and embarrassing her at social functions. For a number of years she had been tolerant of my newspaperman's peccadilloes, and every time I promised not to drink so much the next time, she'd accept my vow. Naturally I'd be good for a while, but the old habit soon would return. She decided on a shock tactic. "Quit drinking or I'll leave you," she announced one morning after the night before.

I knew she meant it, and that stunned me deeply, forcing me finally to face the realities of my drinking and contemplate the reasons for it as well as the consequences if I continued. I thought of seeking professional counseling, the logical first step for a problem drinker who wants to reform. But perhaps I could start by staying home from Riccardo's on Friday nights and avoiding cocktail parties unless Debby was with me to serve as a go-between. Maybe that would take care of the problem.

And, to my wholly undeserved good fortune, it did, and it has for more than fifteen years. Removing the irritant removed the need to drink. And I learned to cope with inescapable social affairs by acknowledging my need for help during them. When possible, Debby would come with me—and still does—to read my lips through the din and "translate" my speech for others while doing the same for me when I cannot understand theirs.

I am not at all certain that my shyness was caused entirely by my deafness and the resultant oversensitivity about my speech. We Kisors have always tended toward aloofness and solitariness. Most of the male members of the family have always hated crowds, preferring small groups for their social lives.

They tend to be inner-directed, caring little what impression they make on the crowd. They also can be irritable and short-tempered. And now that psychologists are beginning to accept heredity as at least as strong a determinant of personality as is environment, perhaps I'm shy and short-fused because my father is, and because his father was, and because (presumably) his father's father was, and so on.

Likewise, perhaps I flirted with alcohol for reasons of social pressure as much as deafness. I became a newspaperman in the 1960s, when it was still considered de rigueur for Chicago newsmen to be able to hold their liquor. The romantic myth of the hard-drinking *Front Page* newsman was a long time dying in Chicago, where it was born. A great many of my contemporaries are now members of Alcoholics Anonymous, and you'd likely recognize some of their names.

Whatever the ultimate cause of my personality quirks, it took a long time to learn to deal with them, especially to appreciate the hard lesson that it is counterproductive to be stiff-neckedly independent. Striving alone means exactly that—and if I did not sometimes seek the help of others in communicating with the hearing, I would be lost in a desert of frustration. Acknowledging my deafness by seeking aid does not diminish me in any way. How easy that is to admit and how difficult it is to accept!

During the waning years of the eighties I made the pleasant discovery that announcing my deafness, rather than letting it hide invisibly with me in the background (a genuine advantage in many situations), can smooth the way in many social encounters. Before taking a long train trip across Canada in early 1989, for example, I decided to perform an experiment. I'd tell everyone to whom I spoke that I was deaf, even before such a simple transaction as ordering a cup of coffee or pleasantly asking the person across the dining-car table from me where he was from and where he was going.

Almost invariably the stewards and train crew treated me with increased attention and politeness, and my fellow travelers in the first-class club car seemed to think the subject of my deafness a welcome diversion from the long and dusty miles across the flat and featureless provinces of Alberta and Saskatchewan. Almost everyone, I discovered, had an Aunt Matilda or Cousin Hubert who was stone deaf but managed very nicely, and maybe this new surgical operation the newspapers were talking about would cure them, and did I know anything about it?

Years ago I would bristle if a stranger made my deafness the topic of the moment. But now I recognize that it's an excellent conversational icebreaker, and that it's very easy to go on to other topics once we've worn out that one. Deafness often still frightens away the ignorant and the self-regarding, and that in itself can be a blessing. The subject, however, has reached such a high level in the popular consciousness—thanks to media coverage of events in the deaf world such as closed captioning, the Gallaudet revolution, and Marlee Matlin's Academy Award —that it tends to whet the curiosity of intelligent and informed hearing people.

I still avoid cocktail parties and all similar large-scale social encounters whenever I can, choosing instead a social life of frequent small dinner parties with two or three other couples. But when there are inescapable social and professional obligations to discharge, I'm no longer embarrassed to ask Debby, or a close friend who has developed a knack for lipreading just from having known me for years, to come along and serve as a go-between over the background noise.

What has surprised me since I made this decision is that the need for help has been so infrequent. My imperfect speech and lip-reading serve me well in everyday life, with my family and at the office. Like almost everyone else, I spend most of my days among friends and co-workers, all of whom I understand without much difficulty and who understand me with equal facility.

Once in a while I'll ask someone to repeat something. In the event of a large group announcement or discussion—rare in a newspaper city room—I'll often ask a co-worker later to fill me in on what was said so that I can be sure I didn't miss anything. Few ever think to volunteer the information unasked, but that's not because they're insensitive. Rather, it's that they are so accustomed to communicating easily with me that it never occurs to them I might need help. At bottom that's a compliment.

And at home communication presents no difficulty, for I've lived with the people there for years, I know their personalities intimately, and I am accustomed to every nuance of their speech. Only when I'm weary after a long day at work or miserable with the flu will my speech and lipreading flag, and a quick repetition will set things back on the track.

Apart from noisy social encounters, I need almost no aid. Of course, lipreading is useless in certain situations—with a public address system, for example. When a group of hearing people are listening to a message from the squawk box, I'm tipped off by the collective intent blankness that sweeps over their faces. I can easily buttonhole one, explain that I am deaf if he is a stranger, and ask to be clued in. Never am I rebuffed.

However we deaf manage to handle our problems, one of the greatest we face is that deep and bitter animosity among ourselves. The world of deafness often seems Balkanized, with a warlord ruling every mountaintop. The old battle between oralism and sign still rages, with periodic skirmishes among specific schools of sign languages. Occasionally I am asked to join the battle, usually on the oralist side. At one time I did. For a two-year period in the early 1970s I spoke to organizations of parents of deaf children, urging them to try to teach their children to speak and lipread rather than use sign language. This was a mistake, I learned to my chagrin when I found myself in the center of the cross fire between stiff-necked oralists and adamant signers. The one tried to use my example, the other to discredit it. Fed up, I called down a pox on both their houses and left the world of the deaf to its own battles.

Since then, of course, I've learned that there are compelling arguments for teaching sign to the prelingually deaf. And if I have learned any wisdom from forty-six years of postlingual deafness, it is that my life cannot and should not serve as a model for that of anyone else. Individual experience and potential varies so greatly that each case of deafness must be judged by itself.

Yet I think I've earned the right to an opinion or two, even if they're not what some people want to hear. Some of them, for instance, insist on asking, "What if you had a deaf child? Would you rely on the oral method?"

The easy answer is "Yes." The honest one is "I don't know. It depends on circumstances."

If a child of ours lost his hearing after acquiring language, as I did, Debby and I would have no hesitation in opting for the purely oral method *if* the child displayed the linguistic precocity that seems to run in my family. We would also seek to make use of residual hearing as much as possible, if the child had any. If the child was born deaf, that would be a much knottier question. That under the right circumstances the oral method can succeed has been proven, however anecdotally, by the example of Ann Percy, among other deaf-born children who grew up as productive and fulfilled members of the hearing culture, using English as their primary language. If our baby was undoubtedly bright and alert, and we could locate a private teacher of the deaf with the gifts of Doris Mirrielees who could live with us, instructing us in the teaching of our child, I'd give considerable thought to this method. We would be committed and confident—and we could afford it.

But if there was any question about the infant's abilities, or if I could not find such a gifted teacher immediately, I'd plunge right into teaching the infant sign—and learning it myself—so that it would acquire language as early as possible. As soon as it was old enough, I'd encourage it to learn speech and lipreading as a second language. I'd give the child every possible chance to become a member of the larger English-speaking community, the same one to which I belong, as well as to the signing culture.

And, in any case, if my child could not master oral communication sufficiently and instead displayed an affinity for the signing world, I'd not swoon in despair. In fact, I'd plunge wholeheartedly with my child into the special culture of the deaf. Though they are perhaps limited in ways the successful oral deaf are not, the signing deaf are just as valuable and productive members of society, their lives just as rich and full as those of the oral deaf.

For the same reason, I wouldn't discourage a successful oral deaf child from learning sign. He may display a talent for languages of all kinds, and that should be encouraged. Being able to walk confidently among both the oral and the signing worlds might give him an advantage the purely oral do not have: another choice among groups with which to socialize.

There is one firm warning I would give every parent of a deaf child: Be wary of ideologues who belittle other methods of communication, and be doubly suspicious of those who declare that the decision on the education of the deaf child belongs wholly to the professionals of special education. Too many such blinkered souls exist. Not long ago I heard about a very bright deaf-born child in a Chicago suburb whose speech and lipreading abilities were phenomenal, thanks in great part to his parents, brilliant and aggressive types who had made his early education their business, favoring the "cued speech" method of communication. That's a little-known but increasingly popular method in which the hearing speaker's hand is held near the mouth so that the fingers can perform special signs, or cues, that substitute for sounds not easily lipread.

This family unfortunately lives in a suburb whose special education establishment has opted completely for sign language. The parents asked that their child be taught with hearing children in regular classes—but the special education teachers refused to entertain the notion. As soon as he entered school, they said, he would learn sign language and be educated with the signing deaf only with that method of communication. *They* were the experts, not the parents, and only they would make the decisions.

This appalling arrogance is also evident elsewhere. At Gallaudet University, several researchers have had promising results in using computers to teach the signing deaf to speak more intelligibly. When a report of their work appeared in *The New York Times*, the story quoted a famous advocate of sign language as disparaging the research, declaring that the researchers' time and money would be better spent improving the students' sign language.

Another vexing problem is that the deaf themselves can be as mulish on the subject as their educators. When my name is mentioned among members of certain organizations for the deaf in the Chicago area, it often is dismissed with the comment: "Henry Kisor doesn't admit his deafness." And that's true by the standards of the New Orthodoxy that has taken over much of the world of the hearing-impaired in the last two decades. To a large number—perhaps the majority—of those who live and work in the world of the deaf, one cannot "admit" one's deafness unless one embraces sign language and joins the deaf culture. Not to do so, they say, is a tragic self-denial that approaches apostasy.

Once again, I agree that for the majority of the deaf, especially the prelingually deaf, signing and identifying oneself with the culture of deafness is the most appropriate course. Those who do so more often than not become productive and happy human beings. No longer are they forced down unrealistic avenues by the stern oralist Old Orthodoxy that demanded they all learn to speak and lipread in order to become successful members of a world that often despises them and would rather forget them.

But it seems difficult, even impossible, for some of the leaders of cultural deaf organizations to recognize that there is a plurality among us. Contrary to the New Orthodoxy, some of us who are born deaf or who lose our hearing early in life do manage to become secure, achieving members of the wider culture while relying only on speech and lipreading for communication. We are few, it is true, but we exist, and we believe our successes every bit worth celebrating as are the advances of the larger world of the deaf. Are we elitist? We must admit we are more fortunate in our circumstances than most. But I for one do not consider myself superior to my signing brothers and sisters. I owe them too much for improving our common lot in the last decade. Why, then, do I not set myself to learning their culture?

For many of us middle-aged oral deaf, taking the considerable time required to learn to sign so that we can join the National

Association of the Deaf makes as much sense as mastering Serbo-Croatian in order to become members of the Sons of Yugoslavia—unless we are deeply interested in that culture. It may be hard for some people to believe, but not to be more than casually interested in the culture of the signing deaf does not mean that we look down upon it.

I'll try an analogy: In the literary profession, the school of "magical realism," which embraces many of the great Latin American novelists, has of late become influential among those who write in English. Magical realism, a kind of fantasy involving elevated language that is grafted onto everyday occurrences, isn't my particular cup of tea. In fact, it puts me to sleep, as it does many other critics. Still, we acknowledge its growing importance among the many postmodern literary movements. It is one of many valuable new ways writers look at the world about them, but it is not the only one.

And so I end this book as I began it, with the uprising at Gallaudet University. The Old Orthodoxy of oral-or-nothing paternalism has died a richly deserved death. But the triumph of the Gallaudet students, who are almost all members of the signing deaf culture, may lead to a widespread enshrinement of that New Orthodoxy we nonmembers find so alarming. As with so many social movements throughout history, the oppressed can become oppressors.

The danger, I believe, is that the signing deaf may attempt to carry their revolution so far that it turns upon them, as the French citizenry, weary of his murderous excess, repudiated the fanatic Robespierre. It has to do with the way members of the deaf culture define themselves. There is a strong movement among them to declare themselves an ethnic culture with a capitalized name, like African-Americans (formerly blacks) and Hispanics. The Deaf world, they say with pride, is founded on a common, established language with its own grammar and syntax, a language that has given birth to a rich visual culture. In short, they define themselves as members of a language-based culture, not as physically handicapped people. In many ways this idea makes sense. It also has the strength of forcing the hearing majority to treat the deaf not as an outcast group but as a legitimately achieving and deserving unit of a pluralist society, just as are, for example, Vietnamese-Americans and Mexican-Americans.

Some of the signing deaf also try hard to communicate with the hearing world on its own terms, learning to speak and to lipread. They seek to move between both cultures, deaf and hearing. Others—perhaps the majority—do not. Achieving intelligibility in speech and learning to lipread accurately is an almost impossible ideal for most prelingually deaf. Hence they prefer to bend their efforts to achievement within the deaf world. If they are going to be segregated from the hearing world, they want it to happen on their terms. They want to control their own lives.

That is a laudable pride. But there is also a certain peril in it: a sometimes bizarre militancy among many of the deaf, especially the young. A short time ago some members of Congress discussed the establishment of a research institute to identify deafness early and to prevent and cure it. Several deaf activists protested that because they are an ethnic group, the government shouldn't seek to cure their ethnicity. "If I had a bulldozer and a gun," a Gallaudet student leader was quoted as saying, "I would destroy all scientific experiments to cure deafness. If I could hear, I would probably take a pencil and poke myself to be deaf again."

This is an advocacy of withdrawal, and it has other manifestations. Many, if not most, deaf organizations have declared that the ideal of mainstreaming deaf pupils in hearing schools has been a failure, that the average seventeen-year-old still reads at a fourth-grade level, just as he did in the bad old days of oralism when he was forbidden to sign. The chief reason for the failure, they say, is that mainstreamed deaf students are forced to make their way in signed English, an artificial language that amounts to pidgin, rather than the American Sign Language they contend is more natural to them. The few mainstreamed students, they add, tend to be lonely because they are rebuffed and ignored by the many hearing pupils, and thus miss participating in many activities that teach social and leadership skills. In a school wholly for the deaf, these organizations contend, pupils compete on equal ground with one another, and thus develop socially and emotionally the same way their peers do. Thus these organizations are demanding that the deaf have their own schools, public and private.

These are powerful arguments. But I am not wholly convinced that the failure, on the average, of the mainstreamed deaf to keep up with their hearing peers is not part of a general failure of American education to serve broad segments of its clientele. It's the rare inner-city *hearing* high school graduate who can read even at a fourth-grade level, and his peers who are bused to schools in middle-class neighborhoods don't do much better. Is a new segregation the solution? Or does the answer lie elsewhere, perhaps in a housecleaning of special education as well as general education? This is a complex and controversial question, and I doubt that another all-or-nothing solution, putting *all* deaf children in residential schools and teaching them American Sign Language, is going to help matters.

Another disagreement in the world of the hearing-impaired revolves around legislation designed to better our lot. Some of the "radicals" among us, for instance, have been demanding strong laws to provide affirmative action in employment. If the deaf are culturally an ethnic group, they contend, preferential treatment laws designed to benefit other disadvantaged groups such as blacks and Hispanics should be extended to them. At first that might sound reasonable, but the skeptics—and I am one of them—point out that affirmative action is supposed to rectify past discrimination, to help once-victimized groups eventually to succeed in society without special assistance. When affirmative action has done what it is intended to, there will no longer be a need for it. What affirmative action for the deaf really means, therefore, is never-ending entitlements for a never-ending disability.

However we define ourselves, we deaf are, for many practical purposes, disabled people. Our lack of functioning ears will always keep us from professions that require hearing. Who among us, for instance, could be an airline pilot, traffic policeman, or radio operator? Affirmative action cannot change that.

What really will help us, in my view, is *anti-discriminatory* legislation such as the Americans with Disabilities Act, which at this writing had breezed through the U.S. Senate and seemed all but certain to be approved by the House of Representatives by the spring of 1990. Next to the Gallaudet revolution, passage of this law promised to be the most important public event of the century for the deaf of America.

I must confess to ambivalent emotions about the act's provisions against discrimination in employment, as well as its sweeping application to all handicaps. It's obviously desirable that employers be prohibited from denying jobs to the handicapped on the basis of disability alone. But the law also obligates employers to provide "reasonable accommodation" to disabled workers, and that makes me uneasy. My deep-seated need for independence leads me to loathe the notion that my employer must spend money on me that would be unnecessary for a hearing employee. To me, that's charity forced by law, and an assault on my dignity.

And the broad language of the act makes me fret that "reasonable accommodation," a concept strongly advocated by the organized deaf community, will in a few notorious cases be taken too far, a danger inherent in many laws of this kind. Let me posit an example: An ambitious veteran book editor at a metropolitan daily who is deaf but oral decides he's bored with desk work and applies for the post of city hall reporter. This job requires hours of telephone work each day, including dictating stories to the rewrite desk as well as frequent shmoozing in the corridors with politicians. The paper's management realizes that the book editor is as knowledgeable about city politics as the hearing reporter who is the other candidate for the post, and that he could acquit himself creditably—if a full-time lipreading and phone interpreter were hired to assist him at $25,000 a year.

Both candidates' talents are equal. But under the provisions of the disabilities act, management cannot deny the deaf editor the job simply because of the cost of accommodating his handicap. There is an escape clause in the act that allows employers to demur because of "undue hardship," but the paper is a big metropolitan daily with a staff of hundreds, and makes a decent profit. To claim undue hardship might result in a messy and expensive disabled-rights lawsuit as well as embarrassing stories in the competition. Therefore the paper reluctantly gives the job to the book editor and hires an interpreter. From then on, of course, relations between management and employee are subtly strained.

In my more cynical moods I ruminate that such a case might make management less enthusiastic about hiring deaf applicants for entry-level jobs, because of costly potential "reasonable accommodation" demands that might lie in the future. Management might hire only a few handicapped employees, just enough to showcase in the front window and demonstrate compliance with the act, however minimal it might be. That happened, and still happens, with the people the Civil Rights Act of 1964 was intended to emancipate.

Is my hypothetical example really as extreme as it seems, a cranky rationalization born of offended pride? Perhaps. But I believe many young deaf people have grown up expecting a good deal of accommodation. From time to time I have exchanged correspondence with hearing-impaired journalism students. Invariably they ask if it was difficult for me to persuade my newspaper to hire an interpreter to help me do my job. When I tell them I have had none, they are astonished. They have gone through their entire grammar school, high school, and college educations with state-financed interpreters in all their classes, and many of them assume that when they go out into the world to work, somebody will hire interpreters to work side by side with them. In professional journalism that's unlikely to happen, I have told them, to their dismay and sometimes anger. Nobody wants to hire two people to do the job of one. Now, in theory at least, the Americans with Disabilities Act makes that possible.

Having unburdened myself of this worst-case scenario, I must concede that in ordinary practice "reasonable accommodations" are more likely than not to be economical and acceptable to all parties, and a farsighted employer who cheerfully accommodates disabled employees can win much goodwill among the handicapped—in fact, it may even be good for business. For instance, the *Sun-Times* voluntarily provides me with the occasional phone help (an average of twenty minutes a day) of an editorial assistant as well as a transcript typist a few times a year. The cost is chicken feed, perhaps $500 a year. The benefit to the paper for this negligible extra expense is a wider range of reliable work from an experienced staffer with a well-known byline.

I've sometimes thought that on some out-of-town assignments, such as conventions and book-awards press conferences, I could use a lipreading interpreter. The paper has told me that it would regard as a reasonable expense the hiring of a local lipreading interpreter for $30 or $35 an hour to help me at a press conference or noisy social gathering for two or three hours. What's more, the paper has said, it wouldn't need the coercion of a federal law. While it'd be reluctant to approve a proposed out-of-town assignment involving the expense of a full-time traveling interpreter for several days—"that would shoot hell out of my editorial budget," my boss said—the paper would be happy to pay for a local interpreter during an author interview. I don't think, however, that I'd take my bosses up on that proposal. Even though I sometimes have trouble understanding my subject, the presence of a third party at an author interview might subtly alter the sometimes fragile friendliness and trust between interviewer and interviewee. I'd rather rely on my unobtrusive little cassette recorder.

I have absolutely no qualms, however, with the act's other major provision for the hearing-impaired: mandating telephone services for the deaf that are functionally equivalent to those provided to the hearing. In fact, it gladdens my heart. At the same rates hearing people pay for voice telephone service, the deaf will be able to enjoy not only TDDs but also "relay services"—specially trained third-party operators who serve as real-time go-betweens for deaf users of TDDs and hearing users of voice equipment.

359

These operators will provide instantaneous "translations" of messages between the deaf and the hearing, much like interpreters in the United Nations.

This service will give me a personal and professional communications flexibility I've never had. I'll be able to use the TDD the *Sun-Times* already provides me to make my own phone calls to reviewers and publishers, and *Sun-Times* readers will be able to reach me personally as well. I won't need to hope that an editorial assistant is instantly available to handle phone calls for me. If I'm alone at home, I'll be able to call for a pizza, order tickets to the ballet, or make medical appointments. That, for me, is the real emancipation of the Americans with Disabilities Act. (It ought to be mentioned that the act also protects the confidentiality of relayed calls. If, for example, I should want to wager on a horse with a nearby bookie, the go-between operator is enjoined by law from tipping off the cops or the tax men.)

Who will pay for these services? The phone companies will, as a normal tax-deductible cost of doing business, and the ultimate bill will be footed by the taxpayer. The yearly cost is expected to be between $250 million and $300 million, or about

$1.20 per American telephone customer per year—hardly an onerous figure, and one that's likely to be somewhat offset by a resulting increase in productivity among deaf workers. It's less an act of charity than an investment that offers the promise of being paid back at least in part—and perhaps in full.

None of these arguments is to say that the deaf don't deserve a few breaks. We do. In many ways we are getting them, from the private sector as well as the public one, and we will continue to push for them. Our earning power is beginning to increase, and far-sighted corporations are slowly learning that establishing goodwill—such as in sponsoring closed captioning of television programs—is a sensible thing to do. Likewise, the more adventurous companies are discovering, is hiring the deaf for jobs they once had been thought unsuited for. If we are realistic about ourselves, we will continue the public and private progress we have made in raising the world's consciousness about us that went so far in the 1980s.

And one way to be realistic is to admit that some of the deaf, thanks to varying talents and temperaments as well as happenstance, can successfully communicate with the world of the hearing. It is not always easy for us to do so, but the hearing also can find it difficult to achieve those linkages, not only with us but among themselves as well. It may not often happen, but when two dissimilar people—one perhaps deaf, one perhaps hearing—manage to share their humanity with one another, it can be a beautiful thing.

Only connect! That was a literary tenet of the English novelist E. M. Forster, who is not much read today, and that's a pity. In his novels he showed how just a modest effort to communicate—to connect—could bridge vast chasms of indifference, bringing together people with little in common on a middle ground of mutual and sympathetic insight and understanding.

For the last forty years, I have visited a single barber in his two-chair shop in neighboring Wilmette. John cut my father's hair and now he shears my sons' mops. He is a man to whom talk is mother's milk; as his scissors snick, he chatters ceaselessly. He cannot bear a conversational vacuum. Nor can he speak to the unresponsive sides and back of my head as he works upon them, but must stop now and then, whirl the chair so that I face him, and ask after my family or inquire about my opinion of a sporting event.

He listens gravely as I reply, nods approvingly or commiseratively as the case may be, and returns to his work. Scarcely two minutes later his face, again thirsting for an exchange, reappears in front of mine with another gentle question. Trimming my sparse shrubbery is a drawn-out affair. Am I impatient? No, for John refuses to let my deafness deprive him of his pleasure. He cuts, and he connects.

ACKNOWLEDGMENTS

Many people helped in the making of this book. Some did research. Some dredged their memories for anecdotes and insights. Others offered suggestions and encouragement when they were most needed. Still others provided valuable comments on the manuscript as it evolved. I thank them all: Mirriel Bedell, William Brashler, Helen Estus Cason, Lamar Cason, Guyeda Cole, Sam Curtis, Steven S. Duke, Mary Everett, Anne Feiler, Dean Garstecki, Paul Golob, Deborah Kisor Guy, Jean Inman, Eugene Kennedy, Hugh Kenner, Deborah Abbott Kisor, Judith Kisor, Manown Kisor, Manown Kisor, Jr., Robert Locher, James McCulloch, M.D., Marjorie Magner, Ann Percy Moores, Mary Bernice Percy, Walker Percy, Claire Peterson, Craig Peterson, Lloyd Sachs, Jack Schnedler, Marcia Schnedler, Charlotte Searl, U.S. Senator Paul Simon, Studs Terkel, Lou Ann

Walker, Arthur W. Wang, Samuel H. Williamson, and Eugene H. Winick.

Special thanks go to the Ragdale Foundation, Lake Forest, Illinois, for providing a sanctuary where the bulk of this book was written.